Edinburgh Review

106 Robin Jenkins

Edinburgh Review

22a Buccleuch Place, Edinburgh, EH8 9LN
tel: 0131 651 1415
Edinburgh.Review@ed.ac.uk

MANAGING EDITOR — Ronald Turnbull
REVIEW EDITORS— Matthew Reason, Alice Ferrebe
PRODUCTION MANAGER — Alexandra Wong
STUDENT BOARD — Ross Alloway, Stephen Carruthers, Alice Ferrebe,
    Katy Mahood, Matthew Reason
EDITORIAL BOARD — Cairns Craig, Kimberly Hutchings, A.L. Kennedy,
    Andrew O'Hagan, Christopher Whyte
COVER DESIGN — Siân Braes
COVER IMAGES — courtesy of Robin Jenkins, Fischer Verlag
LOGO — Alasdair Gray

ISSN 0267 6672
ISBN 1 85933 203 X

PRINTED AND BOUND in the UK by Antony Rowe Ltd.,
    Bumper's Farm, Chippenham, Wiltshire
PUBLISHED by the Centre for the History of Ideas in Scotland,
    University of Edinburgh
SUPPORTED by

THE SCOTTISH ARTS COUNCIL

Editorial

This issue features a collection of essays which is intended as a provisional *Festschrift* to honour one of Scotland's most prolific but underestimated contemporary writers, Robin Jenkins.

A central issue which emerges here is the question: what *kind* of novelist is Jenkins? Different and conflicting responses are given or implied by our contributors. He is customarily viewed as a 'realist', a placing which Manfred Malzahn for example endorses here. Cairns Craig argues a challenge to such a reading, stressing Jenkins' evasions, the frequent uncertainty in his work about *who* is speaking, and his refusals to affirm any single, or perhaps any, order of truth or reality. Deploying an essay by Walter Benjamin, Craig proposes that there is an affinity between Jenkins' fictions and Kafka's, in that both 'are parables for which no interpretive scheme has been provided, or to which all interpretive schemes will prove inadequate'.

We would like to thank Robin Jenkins for giving us permission to publish an extract from his forthcoming novel *Childish Things* to complete this section. It is vintage Jenkins: enjoyable, compassionate, critical, brilliantly funny.

In our poetry section David Clark introduces and translates poetry from Galicia into Scots and English, and Bashabi Fraser considers 'transcultural' poetry, with special reference to work by Scots-Asians. Besides, the Jenkins excerpt, fiction is represented by extracts from a novel by Wolfgang Hilbig, and by a superb story by Lars Saabye Christensen (in translation by Kenneth C. Steven) which develops gently to an unforgettable close and final image.

Hilbig is still almost unknown in these islands, a situation we hope this issue of *Edinburgh Review* will help to rectify. When *Das Provisorium* (*The Interim*) was published in Germany, the heavyweight political-cultural weekly *Die Zeit* spoke of Hilbig's ability to create in the reader 'a state of intoxification with language', and drew attention to Hilbig's dazzling aphorismic talent: 'the novel…contains aphorisms without compare in contemporary German literature'.

The 'C.' of the novel (the invitation to comparison with Kafka is daring) is spending the festive season in a detoxification centre, and thinks of those who are sitting contentedly beside their Christmas trees, opening their parcels of consumer goods. 'The world of the happy is quite different from that of the unhappy.' Wittgenstein's striking remark cannot match the charge of Hilbig's 'happiness is grounded most firmly on the misery of the subjugated'.

(Our thanks to Fischer Verlag for their co-operation and generosity, and also to Isabel Cole, who as well as providing the translation initiated the project.)

The magazine is rounded off as usual by reviews of books selected by our reviews editors.

Alex Thomson has resigned as editor in order to devote himself full-time to an academic career. We would like to thank him for the commitment and imaginative leadership he demonstrated while at *Edinburgh Review*.

Themes in future issues will include theology and justice; nationalism; Scottish philosophy today; and England and the English. We welcome unsolicited essays (3,000-6,000 words) on these and also on other topics. Mid-June is the deadline for receipt of copy for the next issue.

Editor's Review

Fanon, *pas mort?*

David Macey closes his long, fascinating account of the life and work of Frantz Fanon with the words, *Fanon, pas mort.* But he is, as Macey also underlines, now on the whole forgotten, in his native Martinique, in his adopted Algeria, where he is buried—though in both the odd *Rue* or *Lycée Fanon* can be found—, in France, where he studied, worked for a time, and published, and in the USA, where once, in Eldridge Cleaver's famous phrase, 'every brother on a rooftop' could cite Fanon (and where, incidentally, Fanon died, in 1961, at the age of 36). There are both local and general reasons for this neglect. In France, for instance, Fanon is associated above all with the war in Algeria, a delicate subject it is most convenient to ignore. (Astonishingly, it was not until 1999 that this protracted and horrific conflict, which may have cost the lives of more than one million people, was even officially recognised to have been a war rather than a police operation against criminals.) The broad political and ideological causes with which Fanon identified have disappeared, or at least been eclipsed: socialism, and Third Worldism, the doctrine that genuine socialism could and would first be established in less developed countries. But Fanon's commitment to these movements derived from a passionate allegiance to more fundamental causes. It is this which justifies Macey's words.

Fanon was born in 1925, in Martinique, a society which is a relic of

European military imperialism and the slave trade (Fanon's great-grandfather was the son of an African slave; slavery was finally abolished in 1848). The island is now officially decolonised, and dignified within the structures of the French state with the status of *département d'outre-mer*. Its main export is the banana.

No more 'peripheral' place is imaginable. Was Fanon's achievement then due to his escape from colonised backwardness and immersion in the cultural life of France? Fanon himself would no doubt have retorted, in his customary implacable style, that to pose such a question is to betray a European or metropolitan condescension which is complicit with colonialist criminality. And in fact, as Macey shows, not only was Martinique not an intellectual void: Fanon's work elaborates on political and psycho-political themes being developed by Martinicans in the 1940s, for instance in the little magazine *Tropiques*, which was edited by Aime Césaire. Fanon's concerns were, Macey comments, 'profoundly Martinican': far from being 'liberated' from his background, Fanon was conscripted into a native tradition.

The poet and thinker Césaire was a central figure of the period, and incidentally was for a time the young Fanon's French teacher. It is Césaire who seems to have originated the explosive idea that Hitler had simply 'applied to Europe the colonial practices that had previously been applied only to the Arabs of Algeria, the coolies of India and the negroes of Africa'. Fanon echoes this theme in his final book, *The Wretched of the Earth*: 'Nazism turned the whole of Europe into a veritable colony'. If we need to respect Celan's powerfully understated way of referring to the Holocaust—*das was geschah*, that which happened—we need also to attend to what Césaire and Fanon would insist: that that which happened had happened before.

Césaire also anticipated what would become Fanon's most notorious thesis: that the colonised can only overcome humiliation and recover their dignity and self-respect through violent revenge: 'The colonised man liberates himself in and through violence'. The theme of redemptive violence is to be found in a poem of Césaire's, quoted in *The Wretched of the Earth*, in which a slave confronts his master:

> It's you, he said to me very quietly. It was me, it was indeed me,
> I told him, me, the good slave, the faithful slave, the slavish slave...
> I struck a blow and blood flowed; that is the only baptism I can
> remember.

'Education in Martinique was—is—an induction into linguistic and cultural schizophrenia', Macey observes. Fanon was discouraged from speaking Creole at school—for, as one French politician quoted here stated (in 1976), 'it was the French language that brought Martinicans out of the darkness of obscurity and into the light of a universal culture'—and indeed was taught to think of himself as being French, and European. It was only when he moved to France to study that Fanon discovered that this denial of reality, and the efforts to assimilate French culture, had been in vain. For, he learned by bitter personal experience, in the eyes (the literal sense is crucial: in the daily gaze) of most French people he was not a Frenchman. He was a nigger. And the culture he had spent his life learning to respect and attempting to become part of rejected and denigrated him—in its stereotypes, its language, its advertising, its historiography, as backward, inferior, primitive, savage. Fanon's work explores the ideological strategies of European imperialism, which extended, he would soon discover, to such apparently scientific discourses as psychiatry, and the psychic damage they inflict, in the form of shame, a rooted sense of inferiority, and self-hatred.

Macey chides nationalists in developed countries who invoke Fanon in support of their cause, and describes as 'ludicrous' attempts by Bretons, Basques and Quebecois to depict themselves as members of the wretched of the earth. Agreed. But at the same time Fanon's analysis does illuminate processes of cultural subordination and inferiorisation which have existed and exist in what might be called 'core peripheries'. In Scotland, for instance, until not so long ago much historiography could appropriately be analysed in Fanonian terms, as in its depiction of union with England as salvation from backwardness (or even barbarism).

Macey informs us that, although when Fanon took up a psychiatric post in Blida in Algeria in 1953 he was already disillusioned with France and well aware of the hypocrisy and self-delusion involved in European claims about universalism, he was not yet an advocate of revolutionary decolonisation. But in Algeria he would come to know personally European enlightenment's true heart of darkness.

The Algeria to which he moved was a colony marked by stark racial segregation and inequality, with an immiserated native population. And if the purpose of conquest had indeed been to bring a 'universal culture' to the backward and primitive, French endeavour in this regard had failed spectacularly. Macey has unearthed the remarkable statistic that, after more than 130 years of colonial rule, 86% of native Algerian men and 95% of women could not read. The final revolt against these conditions, colonial rule and the settler population (or *pieds noirs*) began with bomb attacks in late 1954. Fanon, whose work would now include treating victims and practitioners of torture, initiated contacts with the FLN shortly thereafter, and then fled Algeria to work as one of the movement's propagandists and public representatives. Stricken with leukemia, he was treated in Moscow, and then Maryland, but died before de Gaulle finally acceded to the FLN's demands and Algerian independence was declared in 1962.

Attempts have been made, as Macey describes, to provide explanations along psychoanalytic lines of Fanon's self-identification as an Algerian, and apparent rejection of his Martinican roots. Fanon disavowed Martinique (in Freudian theory 'disavowal' is a mode of refusal to confront a trauma) because Martinicans, in their failure to combat colonialism, showed themselves to be weak, emasculated; Fanon required identification with the virility and potency of the FLN *maquis*. Like all psychoanalytic interpretation, it is tempting to say, this is more or less interesting, more or less persuasive speculation. There is a simpler explanation. By the time he called himself an Algerian, Fanon wanted above all to fight colonialism, and the main battle against colonialism was being waged in Algeria, not Martinique. There was, anyway, no definitive disavowal of Martinique. The presence of Césaire in *The Wretched of the Earth* has already been mentioned. The title of Fanon's last book (written when he knew he was dying) of course occurs in the *Internationale*, but it is also a phrase that had been used by the Martinican poet Jacques Roumain in a poem Fanon knew called *Sales nègres*:

> And up we rise
> All the wretched of the earth
> All the dispensers of justice
> Marching to attack your barracks
> And your banks
> Like a forest of funeral torches
> To put an end
> Once
> and
> for
> all

To this world
Of *nègres*
Of niggers
Of dirty niggers.

Fanon was an acute analyst of colonialist ideology and the colonised mind, but his idealism blinded him to much of the reality of the Algerian revolution. The important role accorded to women by the FLN was a necessary temporary tactic (for instance, being less likely to be stopped and searched, they were useful as bomb planters), and not, as Fanon believed and wrote, the mark of a deep cultural shift. Also, Fanon took himself to be a spokesman for a movement whose aim was a society where racial, religious and linguistic differences would not matter—in today's parlance, he was a civic nationalist. But Algerian nationalism, FLN rhetoric notwithstanding, was essentially and obviously driven by allegiance to a particular race, religion and language, as the ultimate fate of the *pieds noirs* confirmed: the choice, in Macey's memorable phrase, between the suitcase and the coffin. Algerian nationalism was ethnic nationalism *puro y duro*. What Macey describes as Ernest Gellner's 'sneer' that Fanon was 'for export only' is surely not inaccurate.

One criticism implicit in Macey's biography is that Fanon failed to acknowledge or was insufficiently motivated to learn just how much individual French people had been prepared to risk for him and the Algerian cause. Sartre, for example, the Voltaire of the age, as de Gaulle suggested, lent his prestige to *The Wretched of the Earth* by contributing a preface. For any Frenchman or Frenchwoman to write a preface commending this book in 1961 was an an act of extreme *Zivilcourage*; to write the preface Sartre did—an inflammatory endorsement of Fanon's position—was almost equivalent to signing his own death warrant. (Sartre's flat was in fact bombed.) Despite a difficult personal relationship with Fanon, the philosopher Francis Jeanson aided the FLN's crucial fund-raising activities among France's Algerian immigrant community, ferrying suitcases full of cash around Paris in his car, and became a fugitive from the French criminal justice system.

How is Fanon to be placed, and why, beyond the rarefied academic world of 'postcolonial studies', is he still important?

He has often been categorised as a thinker of the New Left of the 1960s, and thus a marxist. But if he was a marxist, he was a very strange one. He took the peasantry of the Third World and not the proletariat of the industrialised countries to be the vanguard of socialist revolution. It is also hard to see how Fanon's hatred of colonialism could have allowed him to accept the marxist thesis that colonisation can be an instrument of development and progress (Macey recalls that Engels considered the conquest of Algeria 'favourable to the progress of civilisation'). But in any case Fanon's primary commitment was to justice, freedom and equality, a world free of exploitation and oppression. These are not exclusively or in origin marxist ideals.

Fanon's legacy is the commitment to these ideals, and his anger. Macey strikes the appropriate note:

> It is a good time to reread Fanon. Not to hear once more the call for violent revolution, but to recapture the quality of the anger which inspired it....Anger does not in itself produce a political programme for change, but it is perhaps the most basic political emotion. Without it, there is no hope.

Fanonian idealism and anger are now rare, and may well appear quaint, in a society where the dominant traits are complacency, cynicism, obsession with trivia, acquisitiveness, and indifference to the fate of others. David Macey has written a fine, necessary book. Fanon was, is, a necessary man.

(*Frantz Fanon: A Life* is published by Granta.)

Essays on Robin Jenkins

Robin Jenkins
(photograph courtesy of the author)

Robin Jenkins
—A Would-be Realist?

Cairns Craig

There is a mode of criticism—associated with Georg Lukacs and with Raymond Williams—which assumes that the best authors are those who can provide the most complete representation of the totality of their society—especially if that includes the representation of class conflict and the resulting dialectic of historical development. This mode of writing is often contrasted with the narrow perspective adopted by 'experimental' novelists—whether 'modernist' or 'postmodernist'—who limit themselves to a partial or fragmented representation of their society. As Georg Lukacs put it in his preface to *Studies in European Realism* (trans. 1950), the 'classical heritage consists in the great arts which depict man as a whole in the whole of society'. The great work of literature, in other words, is like Marxist philosophy because it 'analyses man as a whole, and contemplates the history of human evolution as a whole' (5).

By such a measure Robin Jenkins would be without peer among twentieth-(and now twenty-first-) century Scottish novelists, for no modern Scottish novelist has presented so many aspects of Scottish society with such incisive concern for its inner conflicts and contradictions. The range of Jenkins's work makes him a modern equivalent, in terms of its social scope, of the great realist writers of the nineteenth century. The characters in his novels range from the abjectly proletarian—the family of Tom Curdie in *The Changeling*—through the professional middle classes—Curdie's teacher, Charlie Forbes is one of Jenkins's many portraits of this class—to the aristocracy whose forests are being preserved in *The Conegatherers*. In location, they range from the tenements of the urban cities (*A Very Scotch Affair*) to the housing estates of the small towns left behind by the Industrial Revolution (*Just Duffy*), from the country retreats of lawyers (*Poverty Castle*) to the villages of the Western Isles (*A Love of Innocence*). Indeed, many of his novels derive their narrative conflict from the transfer of characters between these environments, as in *Fergus Lamont*, whose eponymous hero is born in an urban slum, becomes the gentrified inhabitant of a country castle, and escapes the conflict between these environments to a croft in the Western Isles. Almost uniquely, however, Jenkins has not only written about the internal workings of Scottish society but about the processes of colonial domination by which modern Scotland was insistently shaped. In novels such as *The Holy Tree* and *Dust on the Paw*, he explored the consequences of colonialism in Malaya and Afghanistan, and in *Willie Hogg* he explores both Scottish emigration and the impact of America's cultural colonisation of the modern world.

The geographical and social inclusiveness of his fiction is equally matched by its historical and cultural scope. He has written about almost all aspects of Scotland's twentieth century experiences, from the years before the First World War through to the political conflicts of the 1930s (*Fergus Lamont*) and experiences of the 'home front' in the Second World War (*Guests of War, A Would-be Saint*), from the enclosed world of Scotland in the 1950s and 60s (*A Very Scotch Affair*), to the brutal Thatcherite world of the 1980s (*Just Duffy*). He is also unique, perhaps, in having written Scotland's only serious novels about two of its most significant cultural experiences—football, in *The Thistle and the Grail* and *A Would-be Saint*, and the 1843 Disruption of the Church of Scotland, in *The Awakening of George Darroch*.

Jenkins, in other words, eminently fulfils the requirements expected of the great realist novelists of the nineteenth century. His novels represent the full range of class experiences and dramatise the historical developments of his society, revealing both the cultural specificity of the Scotland that he describes and the profound moral ambiguities that its religious and its secular value systems encounter in dealing with the effects of a capitalist economy in a world dominated by international conflict. In the terms by which Lukacs described Walter Scott, Jenkins 'aims at portraying the totality of national life in its complex interaction between 'above' and 'below'; his vigorous popular character . . . expressed in the fact that 'below' is seen as the material basis and artistic explanation for what happens 'above'.' [*The Historical Novel*, 49] But while for Lukacs the great realists will present the forces in society that generate social progress, Jenkins turns such meliorism on its head: at the heart of all of Jenkins's plots is the conflict between the potential of a socially improving morality—as projected, for instance, by humanist socialism or Christian communitarianism—and the unnegotiable reality of good and evil, both equally resistant to the requirements of the apparent forces of historical 'progress'. In this he is the inheritor of one of the great issues of the Scottish novel from Scott to Stevenson—the issue of whether social improvement is worthy of our commitment if it means we have to outlaw values that we recognise as superior but which we know cannot be incorporated into our evolving social framework. Thus the Jacobites of Scott's *Waverley* and of Stevenson's *The Master of Ballantrae*, who represent such 'outlaw' values, are resurrected in the genealogy of some of Jenkins's most characteristic figures. Fergus Lamont is the kilt-wearing son of working-class parents who assumes that there is no contradiction between writing poetry in Scots and wanting to become an aristocrat; and Charlie Forbes, the downtrodden schoolteacher in *The Changeling,* is also, when on holiday, Prince Charlie, the king of an alternative world no longer subject to the utilitarian requirements of a modern state.

With such range, and such recognition of his place within the Scottish tradition of the novel, it would seem that Jenkins ought to command pride of place among the novelists of the second half of the twentieth century. Such is the position often accorded to him by reviewers, who regularly note that each new novel proves him again to the most important novelist writing about Scotland, but note it with the surprise that reveals how forgotten this fact has become since the publication of his previous novel. The neglect of Jenkins's work is all the more striking in comparison with the prominence that novelists have achieved within Scottish literature in the second half of the twentieth century. Jenkins's almost exact contemporary, Muriel Spark, is regularly hailed, as a result of her refusal of traditional narrative form, as the first postmodernist novelist in Britain, while writers of later generations, such as Alasdair Gray and James Kelman, are credited with finding new modes, in narrative technique and in linguistic resources, for expressing Scottish experience. Jenkins seems to be a novelist whose very strengths are limitations in the context of modernist and postmodernist modes of writing, and whose concerns, however effective in *documenting* the nature of Scottish society, have failed to engage with the *literary* interests of a modern audience.

II

It is, perhaps, precisely the sense of a novelist who conforms to a very traditional—not to say old-fashioned—conception of the novel that has prevented Jenkins achieving the recognition that a body of work as significant as his has deserved. If realism is the mode of the novel that locates us within the accepted definitions of time, space and point of view, then Jenkins's fiction seems to situate itself firmly within that tradition. A typical Jenkins chapter will open:

> It was cold but dry as he set off. Even if he had not been carrying a Bible anyone could have guessed that he was going to church, he was dressed so neatly, smiled so decorously, and walked so carefully. He did not want to arrive with his shoes sullied with mud or dogs' dirt. Most people attending St Stephen's went by car.
>
> (*Just Duffy*, chapter 19; 126)

These are sentences written in classic realist mode: we begin with the environment—'cold but dry'—and move to the social context of the character—churchgoing—with a prospective temporality—'he did not want to arrive . . .'—which shapes our expectations of narrative development. The final sentence establishes a context against which the protagonist's class and material circumstances can be defined. But Jenkins's realism becomes rapidly self-destructive as soon as one looks closely at its operation. In whose point of view is the statement that 'even if he had not been carrying a Bible anyone could have guessed that he was going to church'? Is this the view of a third-person omniscient narrator who is informing us of what we need to know in order to understand the narrative? Or is it free-indirect discourse reflecting Duffy's own perception of how he is perceived—and suggesting, therefore, that his actions are a performance for others' benefit?

In this respect, Jenkins's style might be located as the process that Bakhtin describes as the 'hybridization' of language:

What is hybridization? It is a mixture of two social languages within the limits of a single utterance, an encounter, within the arena of an utterance, between two different linguistic consciousnesses, separated from one another by an epoch, by social differentiation or by some other factor.

Bakhtin's conception has been used extensively to describe what happens in colonial situations where the same sentences in the mouths of the colonisers and the colonised have entirely different significances. Indeed, Homi Bhabha has made of this a central element in the definition of the 'postcolonial':

Hybridity is the name of this displacement of value from symbol to sign that causes the dominant discourse to split along the axis of its power to be representative, authoritative. Hybridity represents the ambivalent 'turn' of the discriminated subject into the terrifying, exorbitant object of paranoid classification—a disturbing questioning of the images and presences of authority.

In Jenkins's fiction there is a similar process of displacement along the 'axis of power': whose 'power' is embodied in sentence, 'Even if he had not been carrying a Bible anyone could have guessed that he was going to the church, he was dressed so neatly, smiled so decorously, and walked so carefully'? The power of the author to assert the truth about 'anyone' in his fictional universe? The power of 'anyone' in that universe who can make evaluative judgements with confidence on the basis of external appearances? The power of Duffy to simulate appearances that will conceal his real intentions in his social world?

Jenkins's sentences are, in Bakhtin's or Bhabha's sense, 'hybrid', and their hybridity opens up contradictions over which neither the author nor the reader has any control. For Bhabha, the hybrid represents the possibility of a double meaning that releases an alternative space, one in which the colonised can assert their values against the values of the coloniser, without having an explicit lanuguage in which to voice those values. It is significant, in this context, that Jenkins was able to translate his moral concerns into the analysis of the world of colonial ambiguity in *The Holy Tree* and *Dust on the Paw*, as though the ambivalences he had been exploring in a Scottish context were in part the consequence of a colonised culture.

But for Jenkins the hybrid is not Bhabha's space of freedom: rather it is the space in which the apparent certainties of different value systems are revealed to be without foundation. The hybrid sentence is the locus for the unresolvable conflicts of contradictory moral systems within which human beings have to operate. George Darroch, confronted for the first time with a woman's naked body, is emblematic of these contradictions when he discovers that, 'As a Christian minister and her husband's friend he had to lower his eyes, as poet and visionary he had to look his fill'. (35)

In effect, Jenkins uses the techniques of traditional realism precisely to subvert the certainties—in terms of point of view and of evaluative judgement—which realism was designed to support. The very minimalism of Jenkins's style generates ambiguities that open up conflicting possibilities from the same apparently straightforward set of words. The dislocating effects of Jenkins's style can be seen in a passage such as the following, from *The Changeling*. Tom Curdie is a working-class child who has been invited to spend a holiday with the middle-class family of his teacher, Charlie Forbes; returning from a day out they discover that Tom's family have arrived to visit him:

> There were four of them. One was a bloated woman in a mauve coat, almost the same shade as Charlie's shorts; it was long in tinker fashion, down to the ankles to save the trouble of clean legs. Those legs were covered in loose, laddered and holey nylons. Where one of the coat buttons was missing a large brass safety-pin took its place. She wore no hat, and her hair, long and lank and rusty with dyes, was arranged in an attempt at fashion and glamour. Since she had teeth missing her leer of welcome seemed menacing and half-witted. Beside her, clinging to her indeed, was a man as small as a dwarf, but at least twenty years her senior. His legs were deformed, so that walking, so simple for chickens even, was for him a heroic labour, harrowing to watch. Perhaps because of his struggles to move from one spot to another no better, his face was almost malevolent. In his hand he held a cap; it looked as frightening as a cudgel as it swung in its contortions. (*The Changeling*, 165)

The passage is a series of apparently realistic details of the scene but it is riddled with evaluative judgments—'in an attempt at fashion'. 'heroic labour', 'almost malevolent'. There is, however, no clear indication as to whose value judgements these are: they may be the judgements of the various characters involved, translated into the 'neutral' voice of the third person narrator, or they may be judgements of the author/narrator himself. The passage suspends itself upon the possibility that it is representing some particular point of view *within* the narrative and the possibility that it is presenting the point of view *of* the narrative, of the omniscient narrator who is constructing the event for us. The third person narrative voice implies a set of fixed moral standards to which we should all subscribe—'her *leer* of welcome'—but which undercuts itself —'*seemed* menacing'—so that it appears to be contrasted with another, alternative perspective in which the seeming menace reveals only the paranoia of the middle classes when confronted by a class of which they have no understanding.

Jenkins's fiction is obsessively concerned with hypocrisy, but it is not the hypocrisy by which his characters say one thing and mean another that is significant; rather it is the hypocrisy of language itself. 'Perhaps because of his struggles to move from one spot to another no better, his face was almost malevolent.' Where do we go in order to discover the truth behind that 'perhaps'? Was it because of his deformity that he had come to look malevolent, or was it not? Is this an explanation, offered by the author, or only a supposition on the past of the characters observing the behaviour of the cripple? The sentence proposes a potential meaning but then refuses to fulfil it. The narrative holds out the possibility of an overarching moral discourse, but then relativises it as simply the point of view of a particular character. In reading these 'hybrid' sentences we are suspended between the apparently absolute moral judgement of a godlike third-person narrator and the relativistic judgements of characters voiced indirectly through the language of third person narration. Hybridity, for Bhabha, is a sign of humanity's freedom to invest the world with new and alternative meanings. Hybridity, for Jenkins, however, is a sign only that sentences, like human beings, are indeterminate; they are 'free' only in the sense that one can never know enough to establish their final meaning. All meaning is suspended upon an endless 'perhaps'.

III

The effects that Jenkins constructs at the level of individual sentences are, equally, reflected in the overall construction of his plots. The apparently realistic mode of his novels, in terms of their local concentration on the physical and temporal context within which his characters operate, is subverted by the fact that his plots are extremely formalised in their play of opposing characters and in their symbolic patterns. Thus Calum, the innocent, misshapen brother in *The Cone-Gatherers* is matched against Duror, the man whose life has been warped by having to support his bedridden wife: the physical deformity of one mirrors the moral deformity of the other, though to Duror's mind it is his wife and Calum who are images of one another. They move in a world which is not simply the environment of a big house in the Scottish countryside in the Second World War: it is a world overhung by a vast 'perhaps' that translates the events of ordinary everyday experience into a different order of explanation. Thus when the aristocratic son, Roderick, encounters Duror in the wood, the language constructs a pattern of double meaning which is both located *within* Roderick's consciousness but also, by its symbolic connections with other parts of the text, seems to require that we treat it as an aspect of the 'real' world that they inhabit:

> When at last, in the gloaming, Duror moved, it was to the stricken boy like a resurrection, darkening incomprehension and deepening despair. From the arms of the tree Duror stepped forth, and stood for a minute in the clearing in front of the hut. It was a minute of cessation. Incalculable in thought and feeling, gigantic in horror, as if indeed newly come from the dead, Duror merely stood. (150)

Duror's apparition is 'like a resurrection' only in the consciousness of the 'stricken boy', but that personal perception is translated into the language of the narrative itself when Duror 'stepped forth' from 'the arms of the tree'. Are the 'arms' in which Duror has been clasped the metaphoric projection of Roderick's intensified consciousness or an authorial metaphor to which we have to accord a more general significance? And to which of these perspectives do we attach 'as if indeed newly come from the dead': is he *indeed* newly come from the dead, or is it only *as if* he has come from the dead? The final clause—'Duror merely stood'—mocks in its 'merely' the metaphorical contexts with which the novel has surrounded its character: moral judgements are affirmed in the first half of the sentence only to be dismissed by the second.

In Jenkins's novels, the effects of a realist style are effaced in the very moment of their presentation—they become the emblems of an alternative level of meaning which operates on an entirely different order of explanation from the explanations of the world of material circumstance which his realism appears to chart. Jenkins's novels come close, in this respect, to Walter Benjamin's account of the strangeness of Kafka's fictions: 'They are not parables, and yet they do not want to be taken at their face value; they lend themselves to quotation and can be told for purposes of clarification. But do we have the doctrine which Kafka's parables interpret and which K.'s postures and the gestures of his animals clarify? It does not exist; all we can say is that here and there we have an allusion to it' (*Illuminations*, 119). Kafka's stories, intensely realistic in their local detail, defy that realism by gesturing to a higher order of meaning of which they are merely emblems—except that the higher of order of meaning can never be stated. They are allegories in form, but whereas allegories require that we have an interpretive schema by which to interpret their parallel allegoric significances, Kafka's allegories come supplied with no interpretive schema. They gesture to a higher order of meaning which always refuses itself, withdraws into mystery. Lukacs uses Benjamin's distinction to identify what he considers to be the flight from realism in the modernist novel: 'Allegory is a problematic genre because it rejects that assumption of an immanent meaning to human existence which . . . is the basis of the traditional art . . . Allegory in modernist literature. . . implies, more or less consciously, the negation of any meaning immanent in the world or in the life of man' (*The Meaning of Contemporary Realism*, 40). Allegory is thus the denial of historical progression; as Benjamin puts it, 'In the light of this vision history appears, not as the gradual realization of the eternal, but as a process of inevitable decay'.

It is in such a context that Jenkins's novels should be read. They are allegories for which no interpretive scheme has been provided, or to which all interpretive schemes will prove inadequate. Jenkins's allegories invoke possible higher orders of meaning—the meanings of traditional religious or mythic symbols, for instance, or of universalisable moral truths—only to negate the authority by which any such invocation of a higher order of meaning could be justified. The title, *Just Duffy*, like many of Jenkins's titles, performs in its ambiguities precisely this invocation and negation of higher orders of meaning. Is Duffy *just* Duffy, an ordinary human being to be explained by the social and material environment into which he has been born? Or is Duffy, who makes war on society because society claims the right to make war, truly representative of a higher order of the 'just' ignored by the mass of humanity? Duffy is like a visitor to earth from an alternative moral universe, his lack of origins—though his mother 'called herself Mrs Duffy he suspected that she had never been married to his father, who had disappeared before Duffy was born' (7)—making his existence a breach in the order of reality. Is he, therefore, not 'just Duffy' but one who is 'justified'? The novel represents the ordinary material world of modern Scotland only by gesturing to the possibility of an alternative world whose spectral presence can never be confirmed but whose absence would render the world 'a process of inevitable decay'.

In the title of another of Jenkins's novels about the 'justified', *A Would-be Saint*, is inscribed the essence of his anti-realistic realism. Gavin Hamilton is a would-be saint—but does the 'would-be' refer to his aspiration to *become* a saint, or to the fact that 'sainthood' is a condition which does not actually exist, being simply part of an exploded myth? Gavin's refusal to compromise with society's values represents the possibility of an alternative order of meaning which modern society has dismissed; at the same time, it is—perhaps—simply stubbornness or pride. How *would* the world *be* if such an alternative order of meaning were real? The novel gestures to its possibility but only from *within* the context in which such alternative orders of meaning remain in the domain of the *would-be,* forever unrealisable:

> They did not envy Gavin. They would never have changed places with him. They would have argued that by accepting the world with all its imperfections they were acting more sanely and compassionately than he. They preferred to take what society had to give them, much of it not particularly noble, like material possessions, but some of it good, like friendship and love. In return they could repay society by trying at least to make it a little less greedy, more just, and less aggressive.
>
> Yet their eagerness to speak to him or just to stand in his presence put a beauty into their faces that had not been there before.
>
> Or so at any rate it seemed to McMillan. (214)

The transfiguration of values that Gavin represents is offered—'just to stand in his presence put a beauty into their faces'—only to be withdrawn—'so at any rate it seemed'. Likewise, Jenkins's realistic texts call for an interpretative scheme in which they can become an allegory fo a higher meaning, but that possibility is proffered only to be stimultaneously erased.

IV

When Marshall Walker, in his *Scottish Literature since 1707*, declares
that he finds Jenkins's novels fulfilling neither as moral realism—'tangential
both to the condition of Scotland and to twentieth-century life more
generally' (321)—nor as narrative because, despite their 'admirable intention',
they are 'oddly static, like a moral fresco in the author's mind' (321-2), he is
appropriately describing but inadequately responding to the complexity of
Jenkins's fiction. Situating Jenkins, as is so often done, in a tradition of
Scottish realism that stems from *The House with the Green Shutters* misses
the point: for Jenkins realism is what is left when ultimate meaning has
been withdrawn from the world: it is the tragic stylistic condition which the
modern novelist must both accept and resist at one and the same moment.
In this sense, Jenkins is not part of a Scottish realist tradition; rather, he is,
like Muriel Spark, a novelist of absolutes which defy the secular realities of
the modern world. Where Muriel Spark, however, has found in Catholicism
an absolute to believe in, Jenkins can find in belief itself only another potential
hypocrisy. For both, however, the novel is the medium through which, in
the words of Spark's *The Ballad of Peckham Rye*, we see reality as if 'as you
might say there were another world than this'. For Spark. the as if points to
the truth beyond the real; for Jenkins it points only to the 'would-be'.
Jenkins may have described more of the *real* Scotland than any other modern
Scottish novelist, but it is to how insignificant the merely real would be that
his fiction bears witness.

The Forgotten Novels of
Robin Jenkins:
A Thematic Survey

Ingibjörg Ágústsdóttir

The period of 1950 to 1975 was Robin Jenkins's most prolific time as a writer. Within this period, he published nineteen out of the twenty-nine works of fiction he has published so far. Regrettably, many of these early novels are not known to readers, and have often been overlooked in critical treatments of Jenkins's work. True, critics such as Glenda Norquay, Douglas Gifford, Bernard Sellin, Manfred Malzahn and Isobel Murray have contributed invaluably to what little there exists of critical material on Jenkins's earlier fiction through their discussions of individual novels like *The Thistle and the Grail* (1954), *The Cone-Gatherers* (1955), *Guests of War* (1956), *The Changeling* (1958), and *A Very Scotch Affair* (1968). However, with the exception of Francis Hart's valuable—but brief—overview of Jenkins's fiction in *The Scottish Novel: A Critical Survey* (1978), many of the novels published between 1950 and 1975 seem to be more or less forgotten. Furthermore, a great number of these novels are unavailable in print today. Thus neither the general reader nor the critic can enjoy texts such as *So Gaily Sings the Lark*, *The Missionaries* (1957), *Love is a Fervent Fire* (1959), *Dust on the Paw* (1961), *The Sardana Dancers* (1964), *The Holy Tree* (1969), *A Toast to the Lord* (1972), and *A Figure of Fun* (1974), without going through a great deal of trouble—perhaps even in vain—looking in second-hand bookshops and libraries. Reprints of these and other texts are clearly needed in order for there to be a major reappraisal of Jenkins's forgotten fiction.

In different ways, the novels listed above, along with other works of the early period, demonstrate the quality and complexity of Jenkins's writing as well as establish his central thematic concerns, such as psychological development and inner struggle, human fallibility and moral ambiguity, the vulnerability of children and the fragile nature of innocence, religion and morality, the question of rural versus urban, the effects of class division, and, in the case of the novels set abroad, the implications of racial prejudice and cultural conflict. At the same time, the thematic range of the early novels, and Jenkins's depth of approach to moral and social issues that are still relevant in our society today, make them accessible and relevant to both specialist readers of Scottish literature and to the general readership.

The aim of this article is to examine some central themes and concerns of Jenkins's early writing. Due to the necessity of limiting my discussion, I will focus mainly on one novel, *A Love of Innocence* (1963), while also referring to other texts for comparison. This complex and sophisticated novel makes a good focal point because it is available in print and therefore easily accessible to interested readers, but has nevertheless received very little critical attention.

A Love of Innocence is one of Jenkins's more ambitious, larger-scale novels. Set in 1960, the novel tells the story of the adoption of two Glaswegian orphans, John and Tom Sneddon, to the island of Calisay (Colonsay). Jealous of his wife's continuous adultery, their father brutally murdered their mother with a hatchet three years previously, and is now in a mental asylum for criminals. The Sneddons' secret gradually becomes known on the island and causes some unease and disruption amongst the islanders. Within this main storyline frame, there are various sub-plots which add further to the depth and complexity of the novel. Jenkins presents a broad range of characters; there are frustrated spinsters, barren wives, religious bigots, and unhappy orphans, most of them reminiscent of similar types of characters in Jenkins's other work. Most important, though, is the story of the affair between Angus McArthur, a dubious but fascinating rogue who lives on Calisay, and Margaret Mathieson, the Child Welfare Officer from Glasgow who accompanies the orphan brothers to their new island home. Their story is presented alongside the Sneddons' and is central to Jenkins's examination of human morality and frustrated sexuality, while the ambiguous moral value of Angus McArthur anticipates later Jenkins creations such as Mungo Niven of *A Very Scotch Affair* and the eponymous hero of *Fergus Lamont* (1979).

As its title indicates, innocence is a central theme in *A Love of Innocence*. Indeed, children are at the centre of the story, and Jenkins's perceptive and compassionate approach to children's ways of thinking is evident here as in his other novels where children are main characters. But there is a dark, disturbing side to the experience of children in the novel, and it is in this context where the ironic significance of the title becomes evident, because the ultimate question posed is how far people will cherish and love the kind of innocence that children represent, when the children in their care are of deprived, dubious, and even criminal parentage. The various reactions of the Calisay inhabitants to John and Tom Sneddon encapsulate this aspect of the narrative very clearly, and the reception of the brothers demonstrates that they are, indeed, an 'experiment in love and faith' (*LOI* 76). Moreover, Jenkins's introduction of the Biblical concept of the sins of the fathers, as well as the narrative preoccupation with heredity, gives a further dimension, religious as well as scientific, to the question of innocence. There are characters, such as Helen Montgomerie, Matron of the Home, and Donald McArthur, the boys' prospective foster father, who believe the sins of the father will be visited upon his children, and therefore that the Sneddon brothers will suffer for their father's crime. Furthermore, the islanders' Free Kirk mentality represents a rigid, even cruel, perspective on morality and sin. This is revealed in the words of an island woman who thinks it essential that Mary McArthur find out the true family background of the Sneddon boys before adopting them. This, Morag argues, is because the boys' real origin will be reflected in their character. Referring to 'the good book' to back up her argument, she says: 'What is bred in the bone cannot be got rid of; what is in the blood must speak' (*LOI* 46). While thus linking scriptural ideology with scientific ideas that argue for the genetic transmission of mental characteristics, the novel consistently questions the moral value of such ideologies. Simultaneously, by juxtaposing various characters and perspectives, each advocating a different view on the Sneddons' innocence, Jenkins emphasises the subjectivity of moral perception. Yet, when the islanders are almost unanimous in their condemnation of Donald McArthur's bigotry as he decides to send the brothers away, the islanders' charity and support is revealed, and the reader is encouraged to view McArthur's religious justification in a critical light.

At the same time, there is some ambiguity in the novel's presentation of innocence. The narrative voice implicitly suggests that the Sneddon boys may in some obscure way be tainted by their father's crime. Moreover, this suggestion carries overtones of the Biblical idea of original sin. Elspeth McDonald, unaware of the boys' history, feels apprehensive about their stay on the island, sensing menace in 'their smallness, their dependence, their very sweetness' (*LOI* 102). Similarly, Janet Lindsay thinks that the brothers 'seemed to lie under some kind of guilt' (*LOI* 107). Does this guilt derive from their father's crime and thus confirm that his sins are indeed visited upon his children, or is it simply a manifestation of all humanity's essentially sinful nature? And if we are all born sinners, can anyone at all be classified as 'innocent'? Jenkins's fiction consistently poses such complex theological and philosophical questions, interrogating basic concepts of the Christian religion as well as the moral nature of humanity. At the same time, Jenkins's approach to these issues is deeply ambivalent. Throughout, his exploration of innocence, as well as his treatment of other issues central to his work, is marked by this kind of ironic ambiguity. For instance, many of Jenkins's characters who are initially presented as 'innocent'—children, youngsters, adults striving to be morally pure in a corrupt society—are ultimately perceived in highly ironic terms. Are characters like Isobel Kinross and Donald Grant (Jenkins's earliest version of a 'would-be saint') of *So Gaily Sings the Lark*, and Agnes Tolmie of *A Toast to the Lord* to be read as 'moral innocents', or are they simply self-deluded, eccentric hypocrites? And in *The Holy Tree*, set in Borneo, Michael Eking, a native youngster set on education and self-advancement, has a certain kind of naivety that almost translates into innocence, despite the fact that he is deceitful and lecherous, and betrays his own brother, a political rebel, to the police.

A Love of Innocence shows Jenkins's concern with the unfairness of class distinction. The Sneddon brothers are unfortunate victims of their social environment and circumstance. After the tragedy of their mother's brutal death, their poverty means that the boys have no choice but to be left in the Orphans' Home. The other children in the Home are also of deprived, even criminal, background, victims of a cruel society in which some people live in luxury while other people starve and have no choice but endure conditions that defy human dignity and comfort. However, the issue of social division and the destructive effects of poverty is kept more in the background here than in some of Jenkins's other novels. *Happy for the Child* and *The Changeling*, for instance, convey a bleak vision of a society which offers meagre joy or fulfilment to those of its inhabitants suffering poverty, unemployment and squalid housing conditions. Both novels emphasise social hypocrisy and interrogate the morals of societies that offer no real alternatives to their dispossessed young people. Child characters such as Sam Gourlay of *Happy for the Child* and Tom Curdie of *The Changeling* are clearly presented as victims of circumstances beyond their own control; they are betrayed innocents driven towards criminality through poverty, other people's distrust, and bad upbringing by bitter and disillusioned parents.

The story of the Sneddons' move from Glasgow to Calisay manifests another theme which is central to Jenkins's early fiction, and this is the question of urban versus rural. It concerns the transition from city to country, a move which is originally presented as beneficial and redeeming for Jenkins's characters, but sometimes turns out otherwise than anticipated. Jenkins's first novel, *So Gaily Sings the Lark*, introduces this theme; David Sutherland leaves his mining job in Lowland Scotland and travels by foot to Argyll where he finds work in forestry. David's journey away from the industrialised city could perhaps be interpreted by some as Jenkins's wish to bring his Scotland towards a 'Golden Age' ideal of rural values like those celebrated to a great degree during the Scottish Literary Renaissance. However, even though life in the country proves satisfying for David himself, Jenkins's portrayal of David's new environment, where poverty, disintegration, and spiritual negligence exist in abundance, shows clearly that Jenkins's perceptions of Scottish society and life transcend by far any depiction of the countryside as being an ideal. Indeed, Jenkins emphasises the significance of David's coal-miner friend, Forsyth, telling David that his escape to Argyll in search of a better life is nothing but a dream, 'an auld Scots dream' (*GSL* 9). Forsyth's perspective suggests that urban Scotland is what the future holds, that there is no way to reverse the process of industrialisation, even though the conditions of an industrialised Scotland may be hard on many people: 'Here's whaur we bide now, here's whaur we must thole it. You'll be back at the coal-face, Davie, wi' the black dust for your tan' (*GSL* 9). David does not return to the city, but Bell McShelvie does in *Guests of War*. The true value and permanence of Langrigg's refreshing influence on her is undermined by the fact that she becomes intolerant of her Gowburgh neighbours' vulgarity and squalor, and by the suggestion that her transformation may simply be based on self-deception. Accepting that Langrigg's power of transfiguration is, after all, transitory and illusory, Bell ultimately sees Gowburgh as her true source of strength and decides to return there.

In *A Love of Innocence*, it is hoped that the horror of the Sneddons'
background will be overcome and forgotten during their stay in the peaceful
and liberating countryside, and therefore it is anticipated that their 'escape'
to Calisay will bring them towards some kind of redemption. As far as the
Sneddons are concerned, Calisay does prove beneficial and refreshing, as
contrasted with the destructive effects on Tom Curdie of his holiday to
Argyll with his teacher in *The Changeling*. Although the Sneddons are
confronted with the reality of their past on Calisay, John's sudden memory
of his father's crime means that the Sneddon story is brought to a conclusion,
as the secret is finally common knowledge and the islanders generally prove
understanding and supportive. But, perhaps paradoxically, the presentation
of Calisay itself conveys a feeling of barrenness and waste, despite all
suggestions of its redemptive power. Not only are there hardly any children
on the island except for adopted Glaswegian orphans, but most of the young
people of Calisay have left or are about to leave, seeking opportunities either
on mainland Scotland or abroad. Also, most of the women on the island are
unable to have children or have never married, their 'fallow' wombs (*LOI*
36) intensifying the image of sterility that is linked with Calisay. Accordingly,
there are clear signs that Calisay is a dying community, and thereby the
problem of depopulation in the Scottish Highlands and Islands is brought
to the fore. The issue of depopulation is also significant when viewed in
relation to the central plot, as it seems that frequent adoptions of orphans
from Glasgow provide the only hope for the survival of Calisay. However,
Jenkins questions the long-term effect of this 'repopulation' by showing
that most of the orphans—except for the Sneddon boys—long to be back in
their native Glasgow. Thus Flora McDonald is last seen with a 'new
understanding' in her eyes after the leader of the orphan gang tells her that
'None of us is [happy here], really. We'd all prefer to be back in Glasgow'
(*LOI* 320).

Related to the portrayal of Calisay as a barren and decaying community
is the question of sexuality and fertility. No other novel by Jenkins reveals
the author's fascination with spinsterhood and repressed sexuality as clearly
as *A Love of Innocence*. Jessie Ogilvie, the schoolmistress on Calisay, has
never married, but despite having succumbed to Angus McArthur's sexual
advances in the past, she tries to suppress her physical desires and feels
profoundly ashamed of her sexuality, which results in her viewing physical
desire and sex as filthy: 'filthiest of all had been, not his hand creeping up
her thigh, nor her allowing it to remain there, but the pleasure it had given

her' (*LOI* 215). There is also Helen Montgomerie, matron of the Home, who is reminiscent of the frustrated and confused Helen Carmichael in *Love is a Fervent Fire*, but Miss Carmichael's sexual starvation drives her insane so that she starts lifting her skirts to passers-by, 'like a small girl finding revenge in her naughtiness' (*LFF* 118). As with Miss Carmichael, there is a clear indication that Miss Montgomerie has been deeply affected by the lifelong suppression of her sexuality. She is trapped within the restraints of her social and her sexual roles; she has a responsible public position as a children's caretaker, but she is also a woman and therefore not easily able to have a sex life without being condemned by her community and her superiors. Jenkins's portrayal of his spinsters emphasises clearly the negative effects of sexual starvation and physical repression, often originating in strict moral codes which are imposed by religious and social ideologies.

On the other hand, in his portrayal of Margaret Mathieson, Jenkins emphasises the power of transfiguration inherent in love and sexual fulfilment. Margaret is released from the prison of loneliness through her affair with Angus McArthur. Although Jenkins's description of Margaret's and Angus's first love-making is highly comical at times, his approach to Margaret's initial frustration and her later blossoming through sexual experience is nevertheless deeply compassionate. Despite Angus's eventual desertion of her, the narrative voice implies that Margaret's transformation from masculine clumsiness to elegant femininity through her love for him is ultimately beneficial to her self-awareness and self-esteem. The power of love is a central theme in many of Jenkins's other novels. In *The Sardana Dancers*, Jonathan Broxmead's love for the Catalan Montserrat brings him towards moments of clarity and truth and is therefore a positive force within his progress towards self-knowledge. In *Love is a Fervent Fire*, a brilliant exploration of sexual psychology, the dynamics of Constance Kilgour's and Hugh Carstares's relationship are laced with the darkness of underlying menace, but the novel nevertheless emphasises that love can be found in many forms and that love, though imperfect, fallible, and often poisoned by selfishness or other negative human characteristics, should always be cherished no matter how limited. Throughout, Jenkins's fiction tells us to accept that our love for one another is always subject to our own fallibility. As Andrew Doig realises in *The Missionaries*: 'Love had to be accepted, in all its shapes; to sift and censor it, and leave out all that was neither respectable nor aesthetic, was to destroy it as an adventure' (*TM* 227).

While Jenkins thus explores a variety of themes through his many types of characters and settings, his focus on the inner development of protagonists is central to his work. Jenkins has commented that he is constantly confronted by the limitations of human nature, or what he sees as 'the burden of being human' (Ágústsdóttir 1999: 21). His fiction confirms this; the theme of human fallibility and moral ambiguity emerges time and again through the actions and psychology of his protagonists. The development of some, such as Andrew Rutherford of *A Thistle and the Grail* and Bell McShelvie of *Guests of War*, is marked by a sense of moral inadequacy, intense self-interrogation, and the tendency to set impossibly high moral standards for themselves. Characters such as these often realise that without accepting their own and others' fallibility, they reject the reality of their own humanity. Accordingly, their way towards self-knowledge and love of mankind depends on ultimate disillusionment and acceptance of their own and others' imperfections. Others, such as Charlie Forbes of *The Changeling*, are eventually—and sometimes tragically—forced to acknowledge that their idealism has been severely misguided, or that their gestures of charity are in reality tainted by the desire to advance themselves socially and morally. In this way, Jenkins consistently emphasises the essentially flawed nature of man, and suggests that moral perfection is unattainable. Moreover, the underlying suggestion in Jenkins's moral questioning is that it is impossible to achieve real goodness in a modern, capitalist world, since not complying with the rules of a materially selfish society would result in social isolation. Therefore, when moral perfection seems to have been achieved in Jenkins's fiction, as in the cases of Calum in *The Cone-Gatherers* and Sammy McShelvie in *Guests of War*, this goodness exists only outside reality and beyond the limits of a socially conditioned world.

I have chosen to call these central characters, through whom Jenkins explores human fallibility and the ambiguous nature of goodness, his 'pilgrims of conscience'. Theirs is a moral pilgrimage, because they usually come to a new moral understanding of themselves and humanity through the course of their story. This applies to Angus McArthur, the main protagonist of *A Love of Innocence*, who is one of Jenkins's most complex and fascinating characters. Angus possesses a peculiar kind of self-mockery and self-understanding already at the beginning of the novel, while he defiantly avoids what he sees as 'the despicable squabble of human existence' (*LOI* 183). Although he does not realise it until later, this detachment means that he is an outcast, excluded from ordinary human affairs, and essentially alone. The most central aspect of his development is his gradual acknowledgement of this exclusion, but also his realisation that his very nature and his inability to change—what Jenkins appropriately terms 'the inescapability from self' (*LOI* 314)—make it impossible to avoid his loneliness. Moreover, Jenkins's portrayal of Angus proves that Jenkins seldom draws clear lines between the moral binaries of good and bad, or right and wrong. The reader's view of Angus gradually changes from dislike into mixed feelings of admiration for this likeable rogue. Initially presented as sexist, manipulative, scheming, and fraudulent in his dealings with women, and as selfish in accepting and liking other people's kindness while secretly despising their human ordinariness, Angus is arguably redeemed by his changed attitude and feelings towards both Margaret Mathieson and Jessie Ogilvie, as well as by the final portrayal of him as an old and unhappy man through the eyes of his niece Flora. Accordingly, although Angus is in some ways the only true villain in the novel, he is also ultimately its only tragic hero.

Jenkins's early novels clearly establish his main concerns as a writer, and considering the complexity and sophistication of Jenkins's approach to the themes discussed in this article, as well as to his other central issues, it is indeed surprising that many of the early novels have been more or less ignored in detailed critical studies of Jenkins's fiction. *A Love of Innocence* is a good example of critical neglect; neither Glenda Norquay, Isobel Murray, nor Douglas Gifford have included this outstanding novel in their otherwise insightful analyses of the novelist's achievement, and any other critical studies which mention *A Love of Innocence* are mainly general in nature (Hart 1978: 278; Morgan 1974: 244; Burgess 1970: 411). Even Cairns Craig's recent book on the modern Scottish novel does injustice to *A Love of Innocence* in claiming that it is one of Jenkins's works which 'explore the destructive consequences of the efforts to integrate the displaced child into a new environment' (Craig 1999: 110). Despite the traumatic shock of John Sneddon, the integration of the Sneddon brothers into Calisay does eventually prove successful despite Craig's assertion. The only detailed and perceptive discussion of *A Love of Innocence* is however to be found in a *TLS* review of 1963, where the anonymous critic concludes by saying that Jenkins's plot is 'as simple and as tortuous as a Grand Master's chess game' (anon 1963: 369). Considering this early enthusiasm for Jenkins's novel, it does seem astonishing how little attention it has received in later years, but perhaps its very complexity and ambiguity provide a clue as to why this is the case. Jenkins is never easy on his readers, he tackles difficult social and moral issues, and consistently reminds his readers of what it is to be a human being. At the same time, readers might at times find his deeply ironic perspective and his seemingly arbitrary use of symbolism difficult to fathom. Even so, these aspects of his work are part of what makes his fiction a challenging process of learning more about Scotland, the world, human nature, and ourselves.

References

Robin Jenkins, *A Love of Innocence,* Edinburgh, 1963. (B&W Publishing, 1994) Abbreviated as *LOI.*
— *Love is a Fervent Fire,* London, 1959. Abbreviated as *LFF.*
— *So Gaily Sings the Lark,* Bath, 1950. (Cedric Chivers Ltd., 1971) Abbreviated as *GSL.*
— *The Missionaries,* London, 1957. Abbreviated as *TM.*
Anonymous, 'Know Thyself', *The Times Literary Supplement,* 24 May 1963: 369.
Ingibjörg Ágústsdóttir, 'A Truthful Scot' (an interview with Robin Jenkins), in *Scotland* 1, Autumn 1999: 13-22.
Moira Burgess, 'Robin Jenkins: A Novelist of Scotland', *Library Review,* vol. 22, no. 8, 1970: 409-412.
Cairns Craig, *The Modern Scottish Novel: Narrative and the National Imagination,* Edinburgh, 1999.
Francis Hart, *The Scottish Novel: A Critical Survey,* London, 1978.
Edwin Morgan, *Essays,* Cheadle Hulme, 1974.

Robin Jenkins' *Poor Angus*: Confessions of a Justified Artist

Gavin Miller

There is a particular kind of Hollywood blockbuster in which the errors and evils of the present are revealed in a not too distant future as steps on the way to an unforeseen destiny. In this kind of film the Earth is liable to be threatened by an asteroid or ruthless aliens, but just as all seems lost, the planet is saved by a Vietnam veteran armed with a nuclear spin-off from the Cold War. Such a hero is likely to be dogged by personal tragedy: alcoholic, divorced, his only child killed in an accident involving a privately held firearm. These global and personal misfortunes conspire, though, to produce the right man in the right place to save the world.

It would be easy to regard this narrative pattern as confined to the mass-culture produced by American cinema and television. The high-cultural artist, however, radiates a similar providential mythology. Jean-Paul Sartre in *Les Mots* reflects on his own sense as a child that he was fated to be as eminent as Rousseau and Bach. Indeed, he recalls that he lived his life as if every incident would eventually be seen as a condition of this destiny by his future biographers:

> Jean-Paul's childhood was like those of Jean-Jacques and Johann Sebastian, and nothing happened to him that was not for the most part a foreshadowing. [...] I was being looked at, from death to birth, by these

children to come whom I could not imagine and to whom I kept sending messages which I could not myself decipher.

The young Jean-Paul's sense of fatalism is shared, no doubt, by many artists, whether successful or aspiring. For 'true' artists, all the suffering they endure, and, what is worse, all the suffering they inflict, are but necessary conditions of a glorious world-historical destiny. Furthermore, since great artists are often celebrated only posthumously, they may never even experience this destiny, but can only hold to it as an article of faith.

Robin Jenkins' novel, *Poor Angus*, explores this belief system through the character of Angus McAllister, an expatriate English teacher who has returned to his home, the Scottish island of Flodday, in order to 'plan master-pieces, as he had longed dreamed of doing.' In order to make this move, he has left behind in East Asia his married lover Fidelia Gomez and her child, Letty. Angus is aware that this might seem rather unfeeling: 'He was remembering his treatment of Fidelia. He had made use of her and then, when it suited him, he had let her down. He did not even know if he had loved her. He was not sure what love was.' Fidelia and her daughter are accordingly now at the mercy of her husband, Enrique Gomez, a Filipino racketeer. Angus suspects, however, that his treatment of Fidelia is not a cruel and avoidable act of his own free will, but a necessary stage in his artistic destiny. Having been suitably inspired by their relationship, he must be free to produce further masterworks: 'Only if he produced masterpieces could such colossal callousness be justified. He had produced one, her portrait. Justification, though, was still far from being achieved.'

While in his cottage at Ardnave, waiting for 'the turning of a competent, worthy, striving painter, [...] into a Master', Angus is joined firstly by Janet Maxwell, and then by Nell Ballantyne, an ex-lover. Janet is attracted by the mythology of Flodday's artist, and hopes to shock Douglas, her unimaginative and philandering husband. Angus is certainly interested in an affair with Janet, but the possibility excites him in a non-sexual way. He reflects, 'Might not an affair with her galvanise him into producing powerful and enigmatic masterpieces? If that happened, no price would be too high to pay'. In this quest, however, for 'sex without responsibility, which every creative artist needed', he knows he runs a risk that has dogged his career:

That had long been a dread of Angus's, that one day when he picked up his brush his hand would have lost not only its cunning but also its power: however much he strove he would not be able to put the brush to canvas. It had already happened two or three times, but only momentarily. Nell, with her coarseness, had brought it about; and Fidelia more so, with her fits of remorse.

A relationship with a woman may not so much inspire Angus, as drag him back into a world where the projected end—namely, his artistic immortality—does not justify the means. This is why he prefers to regard the women around him not as moral agents worthy of respect, but as the living material for his compositions. When Nell arrives, also having fled her husband, and desperate for his help, he sees not a fellow being in distress, but further fuel for his creative fire:

> His artist's mind, never more alert, took note […] of Nell's sudden tears. Poor Nell was not to know that he had not really kissed her but rather whatever goddess it was that inspired painters.

Angus feels especially threatened by the prospect that 'he might want to sleep with Nell. Let that happen and he was doomed as a painter.' This is because, as Janet disapprovingly notes, Nell is largely immune to superstition: 'Nell, simply by being there, took all the magic out of things.' Prolonged exposure to Nell would weaken Angus's own sense of a higher purpose which guides his life and protects him from the consequences of his wrongdoing and callousness. Normally, though, Angus is confident of his future immortality:

> It wasn't spurious second sight like Janet's but artistic instinct which whispered to him that this painting would be a masterpiece. He would have joined the immortals. It behoved him therefore to think kindly of all those not similarly exalted, such as Janet and Nell.

Like one of the Calvinist Elect, Angus regards himself as having been fated to an inescapable immortality. With this sense of election and exaltation, comes an attitude of antinomianism, that other Calvinist tenet. He wonders to himself, as he watches Janet make a difficult climb, 'Was it necessary for an artist to be courageous as a man? If it was, he might as well give up painting. But would Rembrandt, at the age of 43, have scaled the cliff?' Of course, Angus is a metaphorical hero when his creativity is flowing:

'Metaphorically speaking, he could have climbed a cliff ten times as high or faced a hundred fierce bulls. He had had an inspiration for a painting.' This metaphorical courage, though, is indistinguishable, in the everyday world, from simple moral cowardice.

Angus's sense of immortality redeems not only his own moral evil, but also the natural evil attendant upon biological existence. His mother's death is, for example, woven into his personal narrative, where it appears as a necessary condition of his ascendant genius. Her demise directs his life towards Glasgow and its art college.

> He had been born in Kildonan, the island's capital and only town. After his mother's death, when he was ten, he had been taken to Glasgow by his father, a post-office official. In time he had graduated from the Glasgow School of Art, and at the age of 24 had obtained a post as Lecturer in Art at a Teachers' Training College in Basah.

This post, and a severance payment, allow him the money to 'retire to Flodday and plan master-pieces, as he had long dreamed of doing.'

Angus's apparent confidence, however, conceals a repressed knowledge of the truth that—but for chance, co-incidence, and free-will—he might never have come into being at all. This sense of his own contingency strikes him with full force when he follows Janet into a cave mouth at Saligo Bay, the site of an ancient massacre. Legend tells that some of the victims took refuge in the cave, only to be slaughtered by their pursuers. At the mouth is a reminder of the Christian providentialism which persists into the myth of the artistic Elect: 'It was as big as a small church. The ceiling was high. On the wall was written in large white letters: JESUS SAVES. 'Well, he didn't, did he?' muttered Nell.' When Angus is forced deeper into this cave, which is so suffused with traditional reminders of unredeemed evil, he undergoes a spiritual regression back towards his own contingent birth:

> He turned and looked out at the beauty of light and the vastness of space.
> Then, crouching like a foetus, and whimpering, he crept through the hole into a passage where the roof could not have been more than three feet high and the sides were even less than that apart.

He experiences this sense of his own contingency as a loss of the 'immortality' promised to him as an artist, and, therefore, as a consequent return to the primitive, purposeless life forms created by the blind forces of evolution:

> He heard a scream. It came from his own mouth but it was the demons screaming. They were mocking him. Look at him, they were saying, he's no better than a worm and yet he had the arrogance to think himself capable of creating immortal masterpieces. His legs being too weak to support him, he had to get down on to his stomach, like a worm indeed.

In this condition, stripped of his pretensions to artistic immortality, 'he would be like a beetle squashed under a heavy boot' unable to respond if 'bidden to join the celestial throng.'

Angus is therefore upset by the possibility of Fidelia and Letty coming to Flodday precisely because this fortuity is supposed to be ruled out by his predestined immortality: 'He was devastated. Even if Fidelia and Letty did not come, his peace of mind had been destroyed. His godlike confidence in himself was gone.' Their arrival presents an opportunity for morally courageous action: Angus could marry Fidelia, and she could then stay in the United Kingdom with custody of her child. Angus, of course, is a selfish coward, and is unlikely to take this course. Jenkins, though, is a novelist, and must fulfill—albeit sarcastically—our expectations of a 'good plot' in which circumstances conspire to produce a happy resolution. *Poor Angus* therefore ends in an appropriate manner. During a meeting with Gomez and his lawyer, who have also arrived in Flodday, Angus is murdered by Fidelia, who suddenly loses faith in the myth that her suffering will be redeemed by Angus's ascension to artistic immortality:

> Fidelia then, up to that moment passive and meek as a nun in prayer, giving the impression that she was prepared to bear without complaint whatever cross God laid upon her, suddenly sprang to her feet, [and] with a bound reached the blowpipe-spear [...] it was into Angus's own breast that the sharp iron point was plunged.

Angus seems none too perturbed: 'The funny thing was he felt animosity towards no one.' The reason for this acceptance is simple: to be murdered with a blowpipe-spear by the Filipina lover who is preserved in his best painting should be enough to establish his posthumous reputation. Angus can die happy, confident at last of his own artistic immortality.

This ironical conclusion confirms Jenkins's position as one of the most sophisticated of modern Scottish novelists. He offers a neatly plotted resolution to Angus's quest for a miraculous transformation; yet, in so doing, he provides a critique of the myth-making inherent in this novelistic convention. This drives home the central theme of the book—a reminder that truth, goodness, and beauty, are three very different values. Only by spreading falsehood, it seems, can the artist conceal the evil that attends the production of beautiful things.

Where Extremes Meet in Midfield: The Aesthetics of Robin Jenkins

Manfred Malzahn

Consider for a moment the contention that at the root of all 20th-century Scottish literature lies a sense of dissatisfaction with Scottish society and Scottish culture. Vague and voidable as any such generalisation is bound to seem, this particular one could nonetheless serve to highlight characteristic elements in Scottish writing as ways to address, redress, deny or evade an insufficiency of the soil from which it has sprung. Such a classification of different literary modes springing from a common core might help to map out the realm of Scottish literature as a discursive space where fictional statements about the nature, condition, scope, or potential of Scotland, are at the same time statements about the nature, condition, scope, or potential of Scottish art itself.

Since it is no longer quite so unfashionable to talk of literary aesthetics or to go back to the Classical Age for precedents, I may be forgiven for doing both in my attempt to place the fiction of Robin Jenkins into the aforesaid scheme. Let me begin by restating the obvious: working mainly with contemporary Scottish settings and characters, Jenkins largely forgoes the exotic as well as the historical escape route. Operating with a technique for which there is perhaps still no better name than realism, he also forgoes the route which leads from the two-dimensional realist picture to an added mythical or fantastic depth or height. In short, he paints from familiar scenes and models, and produces lifelike representations on a traditional canvas, without any relief or other tricks of the trade.

This choice is apparently made in full awareness of those possible or even necessary limitations to artistic success which go with the restriction of subject matter. An interview published in 1980 records the flat declaration, 'I simply don't think you could get a great novelist out of Scotland.' In another interview printed a good nineteen years later, Jenkins still speaks of Scotland as a 'dull wee place', where nothing really exciting ever happens because 'Everybody is living very amicably together.' The all-pervading Pax Britannica that limits the scale of actual and imaginable events is Every Mac's greatest blessing, but arguably the Scottish artist's greatest curse: especially to the storyteller looking for material, the peaceful *civitas scotorum* 1746 ff. appears as a barren wilderness.

The above is of course an allusion to a famous quote from the Roman author Tacitus. He entered into my perception of Jenkins by sheer coincidence, at a time when my reading of a Jenkins novel alternated with translating chunks of a book on Classical literature. What struck a familiar note there was the portrayal of Tacitus as one of the numerous writers who noted with regret a decline of oratory, and hence of literary standards, under the Roman Emperors. Unlike many others, however, Tacitus regarded this decline as the inevitable consequence of a change which few people would really wish to see reversed, and hence his laments are coupled with remarks which indicate that

> the decay of a great art form, and the loss of a way of achieving individual fame ... is the price that has been paid in exchange for the chance to live safely under the protection of an order which guarantees legal security.

Given his bent to be a literary chronicler of his community, Tacitus saw himself caught in a particular dilemma. Alongside the authors of heroic poetry, historiographers were placed in the highest literary league, comprising writers whom the choice of subject matter and form entitled or obliged to use the sublime style. But if Tacitus looked at the past, as in his Histories, he saw 'a period rich in disasters, frightful in its wars, torn by civil strife, and even in peace full of horrors.' If he turned to the present, as in his *Annals*, his writing was in danger of becoming repetitive and trivial because of the endless series of similar and trivial occurrences it described. Tacitus would throw in complaints such as this: 'My toils are performed in a narrow field, and I harvest no glory.'

Like Jenkins, however, Tacitus went on with his self-appointed task; and like Tacitus, Jenkins developed a distinctive literary aesthetic, which I shall now attempt to document with reference to selected novels. The claim which I would submit is that Jenkins' writing operates within a field governed by contradictory impulses. There is the observer's eagerness to identify with the observed, to show intimate and first-hand knowledge and understanding; this is countered by efforts at distancing, and expressions of a sense of revulsion. Parallel to this tension is the one created by the realist desire to be truthful, to present people, things and events as they are or as they are likely to be, while retaining artistic control of the overall picture; and the naturalist predilection for, as a recent interviewer put it, 'taking things to extremes', or letting a set of characters and circumstances play itself out to an ultimate and inevitable conclusion.

As Jenkins indicated in the abovementioned interview, *Just Duffy* and *A Would-Be Saint* are obvious cases in point. Both Duffy the self-appointed moral crusader, and Gavin Hamilton the non-crusading moralist, are permitted to test the logical or pseudo-logical limits of behaviour based on certain beliefs, before they are finally taken down a respective peg. Hamilton does not die the lonely death of a Saint on a snowy hill, but ends up descending nearer to those fellow-beings from whom he had long climbed away in his search for perfection. Duffy realises that his attempt at self-elevation has caused him to fall below the level of those happy hypocrites he once had looked down upon, and now regards with envious resignation. The greater humanity, it would seem, lies with the greater number, and any form of distinction is achieved at the price of losing touch with the common herd, from which both the sacrificial lamb and the black sheep are detached.

Although Jenkins would in all likelihood deny that he had any such intention, the two tales in question do assume an added significance when read as statements about literature. To avoid too simplistic an equation, however, I would propose to look for the writer figure not among the *dramatis personae*, but to see it as a shadowy gestalt emerging from the dialogic relationship between narrator and main character. Neither Hamilton nor Duffy is a Stephen Dedalus, and Duffy even vandalises books, but he becomes a writer on the wall in order to declare war on the community, and he keeps a notebook in which he records 'every outstanding instance of human depravity' he reads of. Also, he culls the address label for his menetekel to 'defilers of truth and abusers of authority' from a religious pamphlet. Gavin Hamilton tries to live by the New Testament alone, but occasionally perceives people around him in terms of a Walter Scott novel or of a Border ballad. More importantly, though, the two protagonists provide the consciousness through which space for greater good or greater bad is discovered to exist in a humdrum reality with its 'comfortable limitations': or indeed with that fatal 'constriction' of lives which is, according to Ian Crichton Smith, portrayed as the cause of evil in Jenkins' novel *The Cone-Gatherers*.

Not unlike Calum in that book, the protagonist of *Just Duffy* is a person who could be described, with political correctness, as having special needs. When the third-person narrator summarises Duffy's thoughts and perceptions, the reader is drawn towards feeling sympathy for the underdog, and for his fantastic way of getting even with the world that marginalised him. His obsession with housework at first appears as a laudable way of keeping up his self-respect, even if the reader suspects that this cleanliness may indeed be next to fiendishness. It is matched by a linguistic delicacy equally at odds with his surroundings: even the word shit is 'too vulgar' for Duffy, and thus all the strong language in the book comes from other people. As with Gavin Hamilton in *A Would-Be Saint*, the choice of an exceptional central character together with a detached narrator contributes to a style that creates a credible milieu without the linguistic realism that is the stock-in-trade of modern Scottish fiction with similar settings.

Its Callars, Hines or Rentons are allowed by their respective authors to exert much greater dominance over their tales than any Jenkins character can expect. For a start, Jenkins does not much favour those to whom words come easily: the kind of verbal incontinence that either empowers or overwhelms a lot of Irish fiction from Joyce to Flann O'Brien, is not in Jenkins' line. His chosen ones are no slick orators, neither in the street vernacular nor in the anglicised language of the schools. Once again, the authorial stance is best seen as a laborious process, a sequence of temporary mediations between two opposite poles. The following passage from *A Would-Be Saint* illustrates the way in which dialogue and narration interact on a linguistic playing field where there are conflicting rules for verbal moves:

> 'We were frightened your mither wad be wi' you,' muttered Davie, as if to excuse their diffidence. 'Better no' say 'mither', Davie,' said Charlie. 'They'll say 'mother' at Cadzow.' Though they all laughed, including Gavin himself, they were aware of the great difference between 'mither' and 'mother'. In 'mither' was faithfulness to old friends and old customs; in 'mother' could be pretension, conceit, and even betrayal.

Gavin is about to join the toffs at the academy, and to become the lad o' pairts who embodies the Scottish dream of getting on, as well as the Scottish myth of a society that permits everyone to do so. However permeable the membrane, however, achievement or refinement are likely to be regarded as treason by those who remain behind, as well as by those who cross over. To translate this literary statement into a statement about literature: the Scottish writer, if not born a toff and content to die as one, is bound to be walking a tightrope between the demotic and the elitist, trying to avoid the respective pitfalls of patronising fraternisation on the one hand, and the pyrotechnics of vanity on the other.

What must also be taken into account is the nature of the Scottish public, represented in *A Would-Be Saint* by a motley group of conscientious objectors with different backgrounds, from teacher to warehouseman. What they all have in common is an immunity to unaccustomed ways of looking at things or at themselves: not one of them sees the change of circumstances 'as an opportunity to re-examine his motives, beliefs, and purposes.' In other words, they do not want that widening of perspectives which apart from first-hand sensation, perhaps only the vicarious experience offered by literature can bring. The cross-section of the population that Jenkins picks reads like a representative sample group for a pre-election poll: it includes a wide range of different creeds or opinions, which their holders want to remain unchallenged. As the narrator puts it, 'They did not want anything new revealed to them.'

This, then, is what the Scottish artist seems to be up against: and this is what can make the Scottish writer feel just as 'shut out' as Duffy feels at the end of his book, straight after a final epiphany that showed the people around him in a clearer and more mellow light. But, and here is a common feature of the epiphany in modern literature, it is this very understanding of others which makes Duffy more isolated from them than he has ever been before. He likewise appears to lose whatever command of words he had to win friends and influence people, resolving that 'For the rest of his life he would have nothing to say.' Probably for the better, one might add, remembering that Duffy's limited powers of imagination and of rhetoric have made the world no better place, and him the killer of one of his accomplices. Alone in a rubbish dump, he seems even more like a character in a Beckett play, ready perhaps to climb into a bin, or be buried up to the waist in a mound of refuse.

Jenkins, however, creates or reflects absurdity without setting up a theatre of the absurd. His representations of the human condition are furthermore given a locally, socially, and historically defined shape. If you want to see real Beckett types, you can look around wherever you are; if you want to see real Duffys or Hamiltons, you must go to certain places. If there is a Spartan austerity in the fictional worlds of Jenkins which could well remind the reader of Beckett's stage tableaux, then it is still one which has precise coordinates, however universal or timeless it may look. The intrusion of change or history into apparently timeless settings is surely one of Jenkins' favourite motifs: into a locale where life seems to follow patterns that are repetitive, predictable and safe, comes an outside element that upsets the balance. This can be obviously present throughout the whole story, as for example in Guests of War, where the border town of Langrigg faces a group of evacuee women and children as 'invaders'; or it can be almost hidden, as in *Just Duffy*, where anonymous Christian revivalists drop leaflets that provide Duffy with the formula defining the target for his diffuse anger, and so enable him to swing into action with an appropriate battle cry.

In *Poor Angus*, it is a small island in the Sound of Harris whose equilibrium is disturbed by the arrival of strangers, all in the wake of the painter Angus McAllister, almost a stranger himself after a long absence from his native soil. A lad o' sma' pairts, even his modest success in the outside world has made him suspect, and the unconventional nature of his work as well as his dragging back of heathen relics from Eastern regions add to the perception of him as an alien in the place which he would like to regard as his home, and as the most fruitful source of material and inspiration for his art. This would mark him as an author surrogate, but once more, it is the narrator's relationship with him that sets up the textual as well as the metatextual statement; and once more, the relationship unfolds between the opposite poles of sympathy and wry distancing, as in the following passage:

> Whenever he painted it, whether the myriads of flowers on the machair or the puffins on the sea cliffs or the Celtic crosses in the abandoned graveyards, he was trying to convey his love and loyalty, as well as the longings of his soul. It was a pity, therefore, though hardly a surprise, that his fellow islanders dismissed his work as gaudy smudges and him as an eccentric fraud.

In a sense, this island story embraces and comments on all of Jenkins' art and concerns, and might be said to cap his work like *The Tempest* does Shakespeare's. Having said so, I should add that the specific differences are perhaps most telling in this comparison: Angus does not invite the people who come to see him, he is not the master magician, and he is finally killed by one of those whom he had used. But the magic is there, though treated with deadpan matter-of-factness; so is the actual or denied revenge, reconciliation, renewal or reversal of relationships in different surroundings; and so is also the diminishing of the Prospero figure from supreme and selfish puller of strings to one who has to finally let the puppets make up their own script, as he abandons his claim to powers and hence to rights greater than those of others.

Even at the beginning, though, Angus McAllister is but a poor man's Prospero, as he is a poor man's Picasso. He cultivates an air of superiority because the community does not rate him as an artist, and neither does he himself. Popular approval would enable him to be as humble as he feels he should be, but he also feels that popular approval would be the approval of Philistines, and thus hardly desirable. It is nonetheless the veritable Goliath among the Philistines, a golf-playing macho with a sense of beauty that revolves around birds and birdies, who provides the idea for what almost becomes Angus' first truly great painting. Until he produces great paintings, Angus has to surround himself with 'self-protective arrogance'.

This attitude is shown in dialogue as well as summarised and annotated on by the omniscient narrator, in whose account sympathetic summary and distancing comment blend into each other almost imperceptibly. When, for instance, some of Angus' former models are referred to as 'women whose adiposity would have scunnered ordinary men,' the contrast between the Latin and the Scots diction is a telling exposure of Angus' contradictory impulses: to be one from the common people without being one of them. It likewise shows how educated linguistic prudery or coyness battle with the demotic tendency to call a fat one fat, as well as it reveals Angus' belief that the aesthetic quality of art does not necessarily depend on the beauty of the model.

Finally, it gives us a chance to locate the elusive author behind the words he employs, with the unusual ones usually put into the mouths and minds of characters, and the narrator himself positioned somewhere on that middle ground where high and low usage come together. When Robin Jenkins the author comes up with a word like adiposity or fuck, he wants the reader to realise that it is there because it needs to be, and that he as a writer is neither giving himself airs nor being crude. The pleasure in being clever with words that runs Wilde not only in the works of Oscar is as severely restrained as the pleasure in violating linguistic taboos that almost Bookered James Kelman's chances of bagging a major prize. If art, as Freud claimed, is akin to dreams in feeding wish-fulfilment to the artist's deepest and darkest appetites, then Jenkins' deserts are modest and moderate, or he has an Angus-like superego that never lets the words and characters run free: they might, after all, kill the art or even the artist, as does Fidelia in *Poor Angus*.

If Jenkins' words and Jenkins' characters are not allowed to complete escapes from their limitations, their attempted flights create—not unlike in the works of Graham Greene—litmus tests for the extension of the reader's sympathy. In this respect, Jenkins belongs to a realist tradition that goes back to the 19th century, and George Eliot's words from *The Natural History of German Life*, 'We want to be taught to feel ... for the peasant in all his coarse apathy, and the artisan in all his suspicious selfishness' look uncannily like the seed out of which *Poor Angus* grew. What makes the comparison with Graham Greene equally vivid are the rollercoaster rides readers are taken on, as victims become villains and villains become victims: Duffy and Johnny Crosbie in *Just Duffy* are not so far removed from, say, the whisky priest and the mestizo in *The Power and the Glory*.

What mainly distinguishes Jenkins from Greene is the lack of the latter's theological and verbal certainty. For all the moral complexity of Greene's world, it is one where linguistic identities and transcendental points of reference are fixed. In comparison to Jenkins' Cambuslang and rejected Calvinism, Greene's Berkhamstead and adopted Catholicism plainly provide the more stable grandstands for watching the midfield play in ever-new restagings of the classic fixture Good verses Evil. Never mind that Tacitus would have billed it as Virtue verses Vice: it's all the same anyway, if apparently even Glasgow football animosities have their model in a Classical nexus between religious divisions and spectator sports—check the chapter on 'Blue-green allergy' in Matt Ridley's study *The Origins of Virtue*. But that, as they say, is yet another story.

'There was, and perhaps still is, a Christian faith.'

Tony Mathieson

So ends the prefatory note with which Robin Jenkins began *The Missionaries* (1957).   Most of his books are steeped in religion.   Non-Christian faiths occur, especially in his books set in Afghanistan and the Far East, but it is the Christian heritage of Scotland, even for those who do not profess belief, which is the bedrock of his work.   His books are peopled with characters who have a definite stance on religion.   They have their fair share of ministers and priests. Some are Evangelical, such as Frank and Norman in *The Sardana Dancers*. Some are atheists but even those come into contact or conflict with religion. More than that, some of his atheists such as *Willie Hogg* are the most Christ-like figures. His novels are full of references to Christ.

Few of Jenkins's characters are labelled as atheists and then left to get on with their non-belief. They come from a Christian culture and are deeply influenced by Christian thought. Perhaps they even accept that which is humanitarian in Christ. They cannot ignore Christianity, but question it. They discount the existence of God, but spend their lives thinking about Him. Their philosophies usually are not founded on some other rock but are a negation; they amount to a parallel theology, a negative theology. Perhaps it should be termed 'atheology'.

In the Scottish novel, a major religious component is not unique to Jenkins. He is part of the rich literary tradition of Galt, Hogg and Scott; of

Gibbon, Gunn, Brown, Cronin and others who have captured a peculiarly Scottish preoccupation. Not that religious themes are absent from the writings of other cultures. But Scottish fiction may have a disproportionate share of them, in addition to topics which are peculiarly Scottish, such as the times of the Covenanters. What is particularly striking about most of the novels of Robin Jenkins is that is scarcely possible to turn a few pages without encountering a significant mention of religion, whether it be the ominous buildings Siloam and Gantock Kirk (*Fergus Lamont*), atheism and belief (*Willie Hogg* and other works) or portrayals of sectarianism and discrimination (*Guests of War, Just Duffy*).

That religion is a favourite preoccupation of Scots is almost axiomatic. Questions of belief and of sectarianism are deeply ingrained in the national psyche. The truth of this was particularly evident in Jenkins's native Lanarkshire in the mid-twentieth century. It used to be said that religion and politics were two subjects to be avoided in polite conversation. In the west of Scotland, to ask someone's denomination was considered an improper personal question. Visitors from other countries usually have no such reticence and fail to understand why such discussion can lead to offence.

Robin Jenkins is one author from the second half of the twentieth century who stands out for his refusal to shirk discussing religion in public. He is hard on bigotry and on cant. He is equally hard on class, issues of politics, social justice and all the main dividers of society.

Hypocrisy and Genuine belief

Robin Jenkins is deeply concerned with notions of morality and spirituality. Where these are derived from Christian ethics and are sincerely held, he respects and praises them. He has spent a lifetime considering the person of Jesus, his teachings and ministry. But he denounces hypocrites who use the label 'Christianity' to promulgate profoundly unChristian ideas and policies.

Conventional, 'respectable' Christianity, the religion of lip service, identifies as evil a very different set of values and activities than does Jenkins. In *A Toast To The Lord*, following a series of calamities, a minister of the Free Kirk preaches that the people should not be surprised at the devil in their midst when the inhabitants indulge in such ungodly acts as golf or putting on the Sabbath. Jenkins points out the irony that none of the ministers denounces the presence of weapons of mass destruction in the town; indeed, the townspeople are proud that their town has been chosen as the place from which western civilisation is to be defended. It is in defence of that civilisation that the 'missionaries' (*The Missionaries*), a group of law-enforcers, set out to evict peaceable crofters from the island Sollas, at the whim of its rich and powerful owner, Mr Vontin. The title is one of many instances of Jenkins's use of irony. The purpose of the mission is to bring law and order, products of western Christian culture, rather than religion or any of the values which Christ preached. Once again, the respectable is contrasted with the moral.

Many of the novels deal with hypocrisy and humbug. These words and variants of them are found frequently, very often in the context of so-called Christian behaviour. Robert Plenderleith, a Church of Scotland minister in *A Toast to the Lord*, is (unsuccessfully) discouraged from officiating at the funeral of a suicide who had committed a murder, because he should not be seen to be forgiving a murder. His is a 'conventional Christianity that took no risks and therefore wrought no miracles.'

Conventional, respectable Christianity is at odds with the true teachings of Christ. It is this hypocritical travesty of religion which Jenkins deplores. But in *The Missionaries*, the island of Sollas, with its less than conventional Christians, is associated with apparent miracles and coincidences. There is a metaphysical element of the novel which is in contrast to then realism of much of Jenkins's work.

'Respectable' religion is found also in *Guests of War*. A school has been evacuated to Langrigg. The town has two rival ministers, MacDoe and Sandeman. The latter has the most of the 'best' citizens in his congregation. But his Christianity is hollow; when the head teacher is initially billeted with him, the minister badly neglects his duty of hospitality.

Christian Justice

Justice is one of the main themes in Jenkins, and also an important aspect of Christianity in practice. It is therefore not surprising that one of his stories, the opener to *A Far Cry From Bowmore and Other Stories*, is called 'Christian Justice'. Rather than loving and helping his neighbour, a contract teacher sets out to have another teacher sacked for having obtained her post by exaggerating her qualifications. Neither Father Duffy, the

Principal of the school, nor the educational authorities are interested in his clyping, but he is vindictively determined to pursue the case as far as possible, on the ground that it is unjust, and therefore unChristian, to hold a position by deceit. In the end it the complaining teacher whose contract is not renewed. Perhaps that is the real justice.

Christian Justice illustrates an interesting facet of Jenkins's work and that is his naming of characters. There are many intriguing instances of names recurring in the novels and stories. It is Father Duffy who represents the Christian church in 'Christian Justice'. Jenkins uses the name Duffy again in *Just Duffy*, a boy who deals out justice in his own interesting way.

Whereas in Christian Justice the justice being pursued concerns a small number of people, more frequently Jenkins treats the topic of justice on a grander scale than the petty squabbling at a school. He is concerned with rich and poor, as in the wonderfully oxymoronic *Poverty Castle*, in which complex relationships and interactions between the classes are explored. A very well-to-do student visits the home of her room-mate's parents. She is surprised to find how close together the working- class live, as though it were a matter of choice. The working-class girl is unsure about making a reciprocal visit. She fears that after seeing a richer way of life, she will be unable mentally to return to her roots and socialist principles. She imagines herself as part of the richer family A similar idea occurs in *The Changeling*, a boy brought up in the slums is taken on a family holiday by one of his teachers. The boy has the innate wisdom to try not to become too close to a family of which he knows that he is not really a part and which would eventually reject him. At times his resolve wavers and he even once phones home, forgets himself and gives his surname as that of his hosts, to their horror. The holiday is apparently an attempt to emulate the Good Samaritan. Reference to that parable of Christ opens the book, and so the Christian symbolism is explicit. Unfortunately, the eventual outcome of the Samaritan gesture is disastrous.

Poverty is clearly, though not only, a Christian issue. In several of the novels, for example *The Thistle and the Grail*, Christ's comment that 'the poor shall always be with us' is quoted. That is perhaps a profound insight; it is also a challenge. Christ did not say that society should not strive to eradicate poverty. Jenkins exposes the poverty which is a disgrace to society. More importantly, he exposes the attitudes which give rise to and maintain it. Often, such attitudes are shown to be held by those professing Christianity.

Christians at War

Robin Jenkins was born in 1912, and therefore belonged to the generation which lived through two world wars, the Spanish Civil war and many other conflicts. Unlike many authors, he rejected war. Several of the novels deal with the mores of conscientious objectors and their treatment by others, including ministers of the church. Huge moral courage is required to refuse to go to war, yet society often does not recognise this. Instead, it daubs yellow graffiti on the places where the objectors live.

A Would-Be Saint is the story of Gavin Hamilton, a conscientious objector who believes that war is profoundly unChristian. Yet the Reverend McFarquhar, minister of the church where Gavin is superintendent of the Sunday School, tells him that the meek cannot inherit the earth until the war is over. Gavin reasons that after the meek have vanquished the fascists then they would no longer be meek. Conscientious objectors and the relationship between war and Christian values are also considered at length in *The Cone-Gatherers*. The question of whether it is moral, or Christian, to keep nuclear weapons on the Clyde, even as a threat, is the subject of *A Toast to the Lord*.

Conclusion

Robert Jenkins has published nearly thirty novels and collections of short stories over a period of fifty years. They include many recurrent themes, ideas and motifs. Chief among these are justice, peace and religion. They give the reader an insight into the author; a novelist does not spend half a century discussing God and Christianity unless these ideas are very important to him.

Jenkins writes as convincingly about Catholicism, in, for example, *The Expatriates* and *The Sardana Dancers* as he does about Presbyterianism in the magnificent work *The Awakening of George Darroch*. He writes of the interaction, not only in the sense of conflict, between the denominations, and amongst Christianity, communism and atheism. He writes with true respect for the person of Jesus Christ on the cross and the simple goodness of his ideals, while lambasting hypocrisy, humbug and mumbo-jumbo. There is strong evidence of a mind which has wrestled with the important ideas of life, without unquestioning belief but perhaps with a questioning disbelief.

Jenkins's work has a shining integrity. The more you read of it, the more you understand the gestalt. But there is a core of truth which is the essence of his writing and which pervades it, as though the whole of it is present in each published work. That core is human decency, the social and moral teaching of Jesus Christ as practised, not always by those who profess Christianity but often by atheists, agnostics, heathens and adherents of non-Christian faiths.

What Robin Jenkins writes is the thoroughly decent ethos of treating one's neighbour as one's self, which underpins Judaeo-Christian morality. This is a strong characteristic of the Scot and finds its expression in the major Scottish novelists and their characters, irrespective of whether they believe in God or worship Jesus of Nazareth. That ethos is the basis of the yearning for social justice, which is at the heart of Jenkins's work. It is the Sermon on the Mount. We live in a land which is still substantially Christian by culture, if not necessarily by faith. Despite Rachel Hallad's pessimistic view in *A Would-Be Saint*, most believe that we can and should help one other.

The above is only an indication of some of the themes in which Jenkins shows his immense ability. He is probably the most significant fiction writer on religion in Scotland since Lewis Grassic Gibbon. It is the power of his themes, together with mastery of his craft, which makes Robin Jenkins one of the finest novelists of this or any other epoch.

excerpt from *Childish Things*

Robin Jenkins

While waiting for another invitation or summons I took a notion to go downtown and drop into one of the run-down hotels that catered for penurious pensioners and have a chat with some of them. I would go by bus. That would be part of the exercise.

It would be salutary for me after my consorting with the smug, pampered, well-off members of the Club.

On Saturday morning I mentioned at breakfast that I was going downtown.

'If it's anything special you want, Dad,' said Madge, 'College Grave Shopping Centre's a lot nearer.'

'No. I want to go downtown.'

'All right. We'll go with you. Won't we, Frank?'

'Sure will,' said Frank, ever willing to help one who had not yet helped him.

'If you don't mind I'd rather go by myself.'

'Oh.'

Into that small word much suspicion was crammed. Downtown were porno movies, dirty-book shops, massage parlours, and topless bars. Madge had had a letter from Jean. Probably my remark about the whorehouses of Tijuana had been quoted in it.

I had a little lie ready. 'I'd like to go to the Public Library and have a look at some British newspapers. The papers here never have any British news.'

'Are you feeling homesick, Dad?' asked Madge.

'Not particularly.'

'Are you sure you could drive yourself? You'd have to use the freeway.'

'I'm going by bus.'

'Bus?'

She and Frank looked at each other in amazement that quickly turned to horror.

'Why on earth should you go by bus, Dad? If you don't want to drive either Frank or I will take you.'

'Sure will,' said Frank.

'What's wrong with going by bus?' I asked. 'I've travelled in buses at home.'

'It's different here, Dad. Only blacks and poor whites ride the buses. The one you'd have to use takes over an hour and goes through a black district. You'd feel very much out of place. Wouldn't he Frank?'

'Sure would.'

'Out of place among my fellow human beings?'

'You know what we mean.' Madge's voice was sharp.

'I've never been in a city bus myself,' said Frank, 'but I guess it must be an uncomfortable experience. Dangerous, too. You could pick up some disease. Another thing, Dad, people on their own are often mugged in broad daylight downtown, only a few yards from the main street.'

Only a few yards therefore from the business area where his and other banks rose twenty storeys high, the cathedrals of our age.

'You would be the only white person on the bus,' said Madge. 'You'd be surrounded by big fat black women and their screaming piccaninnies. You'd love that.'

In my room getting ready I studied myself in the mirror. Good bone structure. Wide brow. Firm but sensitive mouth. Commanding nose. Abundant white hair. All those are gifts of nature. Who would blame me for practising tilts of the head to achieve the full patrician effect? A champion of the poor and oppressed ought never to be sullen and hangdog. Had not Sir Galahad been the noblest knight, with the most costly caparison?

Making the joke, I heard the rustle in the undergrowth where lurked hideous memories that no shining sword could slay.

I had to walk quarter of a mile to wait for a bus. In that district where every household owned at least two cars few people were ever seen waiting at bus-stops. I was alone therefore. Since the morning was warm and sunny I wore no jacket, only a white open-necked shirt and a pale-blue cashmere pullover, the best that Hawick could produce. My tan slacks were Daks. Drivers of passing cars glanced at me in surprise. If any had stopped to offer me a lift I was prepared to decline with a chuckle, letting it be deduced that I was not travelling by bus because I was poor but for a subtler, more intriguing reason.

At last the bus came. As I stepped on board the driver looked as if he was tempted to advise me to take a taxi. I slipped my nickel and a quarter into the slot and then had a choice of fifty seats, for the bus was empty.

In the black district the houses were smaller, little better than shacks, the shops tawdry, the churches numerous but hardly inspiring. The bus-stops were thronged. A big fat black woman with a heavy shopping bag sat beside me and crushed me against the side. I smiled to show that I did not mind, but she ignored me. They all did. I might as well not have been there. They thought I was being patronising. If they could have afforded to go by car or taxi they would have. Why didn't I? What was my game?

The superabundance of churches—I stopped counting at thirty-five—surely proved true Marx's dictum that religion was the opium of the masses. Every Sunday black preachers would rant about the everlasting glory to come. Their congregations, drugged by that promise, accepted meekly their earthly misery.

In American poverty was a culpable state. The poor were blamed, not pitied. To take help from public funds was as bad as stealing. In Britain too that had been the case thirty years ago. In my I.L.P. days I had played a small part in making society a little more humane.

The bus put me down near Frank's bank, huge as an iceberg, glittering in the sun. I had visited him in it once. It had marble floors and pillars in the main hall, and yet it was only a few minutes' walk from the doss-houses where the winos and drop-outs lived. In his office, with the Stars and Stripes on his desk and a portrait of the President on the wall, Frank worked hard and conscientiously to make more money for his bank and therefore for himself. In his earnest way he had explained that the more he earned the more tax he would pay, thus doing his duty by the poor.

The Reading Room was upstairs. Madge had warned me that its

frequenters would be out-of-work misfits, all men and all shabbily dressed. She was right. Most were elderly. Few had come to read. What was happening in the world or in their own country was no concern of theirs. No one cared whether they existed or not. They stood or sat staring at newspapers or magazines, occasionally they turned a page, but they took nothing in. There was an air of disuse or uselessness about them. In the richest country in the would they had nothing to look forward to. They came here every day because if they did not speak or eat or spit—notices forbade such practices—they would be tolerated. The room was bare and the chairs were hard, but it must have seemed palatial compared with the cubby-holes where they slept.

Another peculiarity of America or at any rate of California was that the old or to use the fashionable euphemism, Senior Citizens, liked to herd together. There were the dingy downtown hotels for those with no other means but their State pensions, and at the other end of the social scale The Ranchos, green oases on the outskirts of the city where retired people with money bought big houses and had every amenity laid on for them, including geriatric golf.

In a corner were racks of newspapers, some from American towns I had never heard of, such as Coos Bay, but there was no *Guardian* or *Telegraph* or *Times*.

To be fair, if an American went into the public library in some Scottish provincial town such as Dundee looking for the *San Diego Tribune* he wasn't likely to find it.

Frank had advised me to ask at the desk. This I did, politely.

My politeness wasn't appreciated. The woman in charge was middle-aged and grey-haired. She looked at me with what seemed disapproval. She thought that a man so well-dressed and well-spoken could afford to buy any newspaper he wanted to read.

'We've only got the London *Times*,' she said, pushing a slip of paper across the counter. 'Write your name and address.'

I did so.

'How many d'you want?'

'Two or three of the latest issues, please.'

'Write three then.' She showed me where.

She took three copies of the *Times* from a shelf behind her,

'Thank you very much,' I said.

'You're welcome.'

I went over to a table at which only one man was sitting. Other tables had four or five at them.

I looked through the newspapers. There was very little news of Scotland.

There was an account of a debate in Parliament on the subject of Devolution. My own view on Home Rule for Scotland was simple. All my life I had wanted Britain to be a socialist country. That I might have hated to live in it, as my daughters and the Druids of Murchison's Tearoom had often taunted, was beside the point. Not that it would ever happen. The English would prevent it. Those lord-lovers would always give the Tories a majority. On its own Scotland might have become socialist, if it had not lost faith in itself. Tamely the Scots had let themselves be cheated out of nationhood.

Absorbed in these reflections I was slow to notice the stink near me, rubbing elbows with me in fact.

The man was as old as myself. There was nothing to be seen to account for the awful smell. It was not simply cloacal. His clothes were shabby but clean enough: they looked as if they had been supplied by the Salvation Army. His face was shrivelled, his hands bony and mottled. There were no visible suppurations, gangrenes, eczemas or oozing boils.

Because its source was unknown somehow made it all the more horrible. It should also have made it more pitiable.

Another man came and sat at the table. After a few seconds he muttered 'Jesus Christ!' and got up and moved.

Illness could humiliate. The poor fellow must know that he exuded this stench of decay, disease, and mortality. Where could he go that it would not offend anyone? There were many such places in California with its enormous deserts, but perhaps he needed the company of people, even of people who could not bear his presence.

There were notices enjoining silence, but surely no committee framing rules and no woman appointed to see that they were observed would have objected to a whispered: 'What is wrong, friend? Is there anything I can do to help?'

I did not say it. Instead I tried to read a witty article on the badness of food in British roadside restaurants.

Two men at the counter were talking to the attendant and looking in the direction of my companion. They were protesting about his presence.

I wished the unfortunate man would go of his own accord and spare everyone the unpleasantness of seeing him ordered out.

The attendant came over and stood beside us. Her nose twitched. In this land of gadgets there was none to assess the amount of human stink allowable in a public library.

On her dour face appeared for a few seconds a gentleness of pity.

He got up and crept out of the room, with a shame and weariness poignant to behold.

'If I get complaints,' she said, 'I've got to act on them. Was he bothering you?'

She did not wait for an answer. It was as well, for it would have taken me a long time to find one.

Out on the street I did not now have the impudence to venture into a pensioners' hotel with my dubious solicitude.

All of me shaky, especially my legs, I went into the first bar I came to. I almost ran out again for it had a juke-box blaring pop music and barmaids with bare bosoms, but I slunk over and crouched in a corner.

The girl who swaggered over to take my order was chewing gum. She had hard eyes, dyed blonde hair, and big breasts, but she was young and healthy and smelled like roses. I could not resist sniffing gratefully.

How could I have explained to her that she represented, not a means of stimulating enfeebled lust, but the sweetness and goodness of life itself? Alas, she misinterpreted my sniffing. No doubt in the hope of a tip made generous by guilt she let her left breast touch my cheek as she bent down to wipe the table.

'Smell all you want, Grandpa,' she said.

I had meant to order beer for it was too early for whisky but I found myself whimpering, 'A Scotch, please, with water.'

'You foreign? Where from? Let me guess. Poland?'

I shook my head.

'Ireland?'

This time I nodded. Let Ireland be given the discredit of the sniffing old lecher.

'It'll be Irish whiskey then?'

I nodded.

When she came back with the whiskey I gave her a dollar as a tip. It was more than generous, but she seemed displeased. She thought I should have paid for the sniffs.

I took the taxi home, though it cost twenty dollars.

Galicia: An Iberian Caledonia?

David M. Clark

With the optimism of the restoration of the Scottish Parliament, many Scots look towards other small counties which, like Norway or Holland, are independent within the wider context of the European Union, or towards other 'stateless nations' whose political and cultural situations resemble that of Scotland. Catalonia is one of the most widely admired models—a part of, yet apart from, the Spanish state—and the fact that Catalonia has controlled a large part of her internal affairs since the fall of Franco's dictatorship has attracted a large amount of Scottish interest. The buoyant Catalan cultural scene and the extremely successful defence of the Catalan language has certainly produced a generation of Catalans who consider themselves to be more Catalan than Spanish, and the cultural independence of Catalonia would appear to be assured for the foreseeable future.

It must be remembered, however, that Catalonia is one of the three so-called historical 'nations' which co-exist with the larger grouping of autonomous communities in Spain. 'Historical' communities are those which received their Statute of Autonomy before the fascist coup in 1936, and as well as Catalonia these consist of the Basque Country (Euskadi) and Galicia. This latter territory, in the rainy north-west corner of the Peninsula, is the least known of the three but, despite the lack of apparent connections, Galicia very probably possesses, in terms of culture, language and geography, much more in common with Scotland than many other small European nations.

The Galician connection with Scotland is, according to legend, rooted in the pre-history of the respective nations. According to the Irish Leabhar Gabhála, the Book of Invasions, the sons of the Galician King Brogan settled in Ireland after their father had spied the Western Island from atop his Tower. With them the sons of Breogan took the stone Jacob had used as pillow when he dreamt of his ladder, and on which Galician—and later Irish—kings were crowned. Legend further has it that, when the Irish Scots travelled to Scotland, they took this stone with them, where it was still used as the throne for Scottish monarchs, passing into history as the Scone Stone, the Stone of Destiny, now an icon of Scottish nationalism.

In more recent times, Scotland has been highly influential in the resurgence of Galician nationalism. In the mid-nineteenth century Eduardo Pondal sought in the works of James MacPherson's 'Ossian' poems to 'recreate' an idealised Celtic Galicia of the past, in which bards, druids and warriors carried out their legendary struggles under a persistent northern mist. The current Galician national anthem is, in fact, based on one of Pondal's poems, and is highly reminiscent of much of the work of the 'Ossian' poet.

The incipient Celticism of Pondal was used by many of the later 19th century nationalists to project a differentiated image of Galicia—if Spain was to look for her national identity in a Mediterranean past, Galicia would look to Scotland and to Ireland. Not for nothing are the Galician bagpipes the traditional national instrument. Significantly, Galicia's national bard, Rosalía de Castro, is as important in the Galician national psyche as Burns in the Scottish.

The early regionalists of the 19th century gave way to a new, more forceful nationalism at the beginning of the 20th century. The '*Irmandades da Falà*' (Brotherhood of the Language), founded in 1916, believed that Galician nationhood could only be recuperated through a defence of the vernacular Galician language, the ancestor of modern Portuguese. The fact that both Castilian Spanish and Galician are Romance languages meant that with Madrid-based hegemony Galician lost much of its social prestige and, like Scots following the Union, was regarded by many as being not a separate language but rather an 'incorrect' variant of the more socially prestigious tongue. Thus the relationship between Galician and Spanish was comparable to that between Scots and English. This, perhaps surprisingly, is in stark contrast with the situation in Catalonia, where the vernacular has been traditionally defended by the native bourgeoisie.

Galician nationalism reached its most creative level with the '*Nós*' generation of writers which lasted from 1924 until the outbreak of civil war in 1936. These writers—including Castelao, Otero Pedrayo and Vicente Risco, loosely grouped around the magazine *Nós*—created a startlingly effusive output of literature in Galician in the form of novels, poems, essays and translations. Interestingly, this generation of writers coincided almost exactly in time with the most fecund period of the Scottish literary renaissance, and the two movements had much in common. So much so, that to read some of Neil Gunn's late 20s and early 30s articles in the *Scots Magazine* is almost like reading Risco in *Nós*. Both groups looked to Ireland for political and cultural inspiration, and both groups disappeared—in the Galician case, directly, in the Scottish case, indirectly—when faced with the threat of fascism.

After the Civil War, Galician nationalism was kept alive largely amongst Galician emigrants in South America. Like Scotland, Galicia has traditionally been a nation of emigrants, and the Galician Cultural Circles in cities such as Buenos Aires helped to keep Galician language and culture alive during the 'lang nicht o' stane'—the seemingly interminable Franco regime. In 1962 Celso Emilio Ferreiro published his clandestine *Longa noite de pedra*, a selection of poems which were to echo the frustration and discontent of a new generation of Galician nationalists, which developed its political wing with the creation of the UPG (Galician People's Union) in 1964, supported by influential young writers like Xosé L. Méndez Ferrín. Franco had banned Galician from schools and all levels of public life, but the language survived in the countryside and among dissenting intellectual circles.

After the fall of Franco, and the long-awaited inauguration of the Galician Parliament (*A Xunta*), the Galician language began to flourish once again. Galician is now the official language in courts, schools, universities and at all levels of public administration. Young novelists like Suso de Toro and Manuel Rivas, and poets such as Xulio Valcárcel, Miguel Anxo Fernán Vello and Pilar Pallarés are creating a dynamic literary scene which, as in the 20s and 30s, coincides surprisingly with the cultural situation in Scotland.

Poems from Galicia

translated by David M. Clark

Celso Emilio Ferreiro

TIME TAE GREET

Ah maun greet sair wi'oot tears
Fir the gulliegawed doos o the licht
Fir the baiten smeddum o the nicht
O hure-sault leeberty.
The swurds hing seelent
Lik cauld weet afore the een
An' ah maun greet i the flichtit shedda
O this smeekie wund
Whilk smores the leal an cheens
The herts o guidwillie men.

But ainly ma een hae latten me
Greet lang burns o tears,
An ah maun sail lang vaiges, nae shalter
Fae times tae cum, times full o scum,
Fae whaur the day taks on
Fae whaur the new warld breirs.

Fir he wha greets, leeves; we wull cairry on,
Cairry on, greetin', shankin'
Wir gallus voice maun brak wi' rage
A gullie o rowst an' stramash
Tae owercome the laithfu' dunts.

A' time maun hae its time
An' this is the time fir greetin'.

LANG NICHT O STANE

The ruif is makkit o stane.
Stane the was
An' the mirkness.
Stane the flair
An' the stainchels.
The duirs,
The cheens,
The smore,
The winnocks,
The glents
Are makkit o stane.
The herts o the fowk
Keekin' slee fae yonder
Forby
Are makkit o stane.
An' me, ah'm deein'
I this lang nicht o stane.

Miguel Anxo Fernán-Vello

THE JOURNEY
To Jordi Virallonga

I would like, in this poem, to let the flower of distance fall,
Blue, over me, now that I depart and leave behind the sea
And a dark land finds in my blood
The old road of sadness.

I am heading south. I crave to find the sweet direction of other days,
The white light of other bodies.
I am abandoning the ash and the poverty of these times,
Tied to men and women in a strange city
Like the desolate wind which blows through its streets.

I live among barbarians and each horizon brings relief.

That is why I bid farewell to the last tree
And in my eyes, like a blade of astonishment
Remains the kiss of the rain and the dusk.

Because I must unveil a new state of health
To light up in the coming months the homeland of desire
And I must let roots grow with the thirst of a star.

I know that all destiny is a strange alliance
Between emptiness, nothingness and a secret which shines
In my heart.

And I give myself up to that light, naked and burned,
The passion of the dawn, profile of a sky which trembles
In these lines which flee, like a dream,
From time and from death.

HEADING NORTH

What is there in this wind that makes the light tremble
And shakes the glass heart of distance
With a blow pronounced by salt-bitter lips
Over the lands which arise giving trees to the morning?
We know the sea is behind the green plains
Where stone is the limit
And the sky sheds a tear of freshness.

On the road there is a feeling which grows in silence
In the well, which we feel like a snowdrop
Slowly opening within our body.

Feeling distance in our blood,
Touching the hidden knot of time,
Drinking from the root that lights up our eyes.

The maps of hope show another life.
Now we have left behind the last impure street
The vile commerce which perturbs the city.
Now this verse knows there is another, higher, light
And an echo of desire quivers within its being.
This journey to the north is an expected miracle,
The perfect escape towards the sea, a destiny
Which we carry, written like a winter gleam
On the homeland of our solitude.

Xavier Rodríguez Baixeras

NORTH SHORE

From you I took the sea-change
The silent steps to nowhere
The freed voice of childhood
Your desolate face.

Before I donned my city helmet
Before I entered the hidden chambers, before I got lost
In bitten alleys, I loved
Your desolate face.

For years I wandered aimlessly between walls
Afraid of all the waves that embrace you
And in which, you, accidentally, prolong
Your desolate face.

But now I detect a light
Of pity in the eyes of the absent ones
Because my life continues and does not erase
Your desolate face.

That this hand might belong to it, the fantasy
You hide in your luminous folds
The delight of the birds when they cross it
Sleepless, in a murmur.

THE DAUGHTER OF MY JOURNEY

Aina, perhaps the sweetest thing in life
Is not to feel calm about a parting,
Not to sleep that night, to be afraid of yourself,
But also of other people, dangerous and proud.

Leave everything in the corridor of a train
—never with resentment, never feeling hunted—
and in the waiting rooms watch the waves
of another sea break, and change horizons every day.

Feel the beauty of distance, the deep
Sadness of a light bulb in the night, the pleasure
Of this immense city which drags you in and blinds you.

Never again to break up, go back to search for yourself
In the alleys of the night and the beaches of the dawn,
And the strength to return and not be the same as before.

Xosé María Álvarez Cáccamo

from **ARCHITECTURE OF ASH**

Let time be always the motionless evening
The oblique light held keeping bodies together,
Helping to readily forget. Let the serene sea move on
Gathering the excess and closing in the shadows.
Let the hours remain in the difficult memory
Of one who has drunk wine from mirrored vineyards
Woven by bees. Let the mother be ours always
Comforting us all with the trace of words
Talking to each child in a different voice.

Let death be later the reported meeting
Of everyone around the white table in the shade
Under the russet leaves drawn by the living light
And in the centre a jar of peaceful wine
Imitating the form of the sun when September grows.

from **CHRONICLE OF HORROR**

The letters that read 'I'll always remain within you
Just as I promised', 'Do not let my children
feel ashamed about my death', 'Do not let my killers
Go unforgotten.'

Words which were dreamt against the walls of wind,
An impossible defence against the law of extermination:
'If the court deems that my love for my homeland
Be sufficient reason for the taking of my life,
I will die for Galicia.'

The unequivocal sentence, the programme of death,
A thistle of blue fire. History built
On the ash of skulls.

History has been moulded from the clay of terror
And on the very foundations of crime
They have built their houses and their families
Ministers   officials   priests   mayors
Secretaries   inspectors   police
Bureaucrats   bankers   soldiers
Assassins   assassins   assassins.

On top of fifty layers of massacred bones,
Over the dry stream where the blood flowed,
On the peak of the rubbish-heap of broken hours,
On the summit of the temples of a lament which never ceased
The ignoble house was built, its walls of black whitewash
Led by the beast
Who calculated, by the light of a candle-lit altar,
The duration of disconsolate death, the total weight of the smashed
corpses,
The definitive path of loss, the infinite direction of sadness, the profits
of terror.

Foundations
For the construction of an ignoble house, built
On top of the flame of fifty
Layers of corpses.

Do Continents Merge?
A reading of poems by some
contemporary Scottish writers

Bashabi Fraser

At an Exhibition on the presence of ethnic minorities in Britain and their contribution to British diversity, there was a banner which encapsulated the whole post-Empire experience: 'We are here because you were there'. The Scots have been known for their *Wanderlust* as they have travelled to America, Africa, the West Indies, India and Australia; wherever the British set up their colonies. It is because the Scots were 'there' that links were established which brought the people of those lands 'here'. However, for many Scots, the Empire experience is valid in a different way, as they have felt that Scotland has been an undeclared 'colony' of the British Empire. Given the Eton/Harrow-Oxbridge/Sandhurst background of those who ruled the colonies, it was the English who largely ruled the Empire as administrators and military officials, while the Scots served the Empire as professionals like their Irish, Welsh, Canadian and Indian counterparts. So the colonial experience is, in a sense, shared by the ex-colonized and the Scots. It is in this context that one can draw parallels in experience and read the poetry of today's Scots as voicing a shared experience in an emerging multi-cultural country.

This article looks at the reality of deictics for a writer today in Scotland and explores the question of identity, place and space, of location and dislocation, of the sense of proximity and distance and of groping for and finding a point of reference in poetry which reflects a dual experience of two cultures and/or languages. Poems which look for 'Scotlands of the mind' are analysed to see if 'continents' do indeed merge in the imagination of the poet.

The poems referred to are from two anthologies of poetry that were published last August in Edinburgh, which epitomise what is happening in Scottish poetry today. The volumes are: *Wish I Was Here*, edited by Kevin MacNeil and Alec Finlay, and *Edinburgh: An Intimate City*, edited by Bashabi Fraser and Elaine Greig. Henceforth the two book will be referred to as *WIWH* and *EAIC*, respectively.

Some lines from a poem by a visitor to Scotland sum up the reality of the colonial experience for old and new Scots:

Namaskar, Sir Walter, I bring greetings from both my Dadus
grandfathers from the Raj,…
No two Dadus were so unlike, but your brave words lit up their shelves;
They roamed with you in the craggy Highlands, the buzzing Borders,
The great castles and, of course, the regal streets of Edinburgh.
Courteous Timarpur Dadu had worked in Defence and earned a title….
I … ruffled his snowy hair, pronouncing him 'a lovely boy'—my
Ivanhoe….
Mussoorie Dadu…gave me poems of passion
And adventure - a free soul, my wild Gallic Rover, my young Lochinvar.

Having roamed with you in the craggy Highlands, the buzzing Borders,
The great castles and, of course, the regal streets of Edinburgh,
I stand at last before your statue. Namaskar, Sir Walter,
From the bottom of my heart. Please accept my Indian greetings.
(Debjani Chatterjee's 'Namaskar, Sir Walter Scott' in *EAIC*)

This is the position many writers share with Debjani, having been introduced to the romance of Scotland and its history through its literature on the shelves of grandfathers, sometimes even before they came to Scotland. It also echoes the legacy of the Raj, of shared tales, loves and experiences.

Just as the Scots left Scotland to settle elsewhere or serve the Empire, the people from the countries they travelled to, came and settled here. In Scotland, the encounter of different cultures has often been embodied with an unbridgeable gap between people:

A woman passed round me
In a slow watchful circle, as if I were a superstition;

Or the worst dregs of her imagination,...
Her words spliced into bars
Of an old wheel....
Where do you come from?
'Here,' I said, 'Here. These parts.'
(Jackie Kay, 'In my country', in *WIWH*)

Jackie Kay's answer reads almost like an apology to a question that writers confront many a time from people who assume that they are only ephemeral visitors to Scotland, who cannot understand that they are 'here' to stay because *they* were once 'there'.

Another poem, which does not appear in the two volumes under discussion, does, however, voice this problem of blending in:

A city is your city when it
Does not look for a
Camera round your neck
And expect you to stand
Map in hand, undecided
On the kerb, with a faltering
Smile—an island—avoiding which,
Its populace flows unconcerned.

A city is your city when it
Does not view you
As a curious interloper
Indulging your sense of indirection
Assuming you have lost your way
Having strayed beyond your
Confines, tolerated temporarily
As an ephemeral guest.

The sense of alienation can be driven home more strongly by racism:

The one saying
You have no street
You have no town
Your voice is nothing I know
Is the one who pushed the burning rag
through the letterbox
You have no voice
Your voice is nothing...
(—as expressed by Gerrie Fellows, who is from New Zealand, in 'At the
Alien's Gate', in *WIWH*).

One frequently comes across the feeling of uprootedness in poems by
trans-cultural writers, which results in a sense of disorientation evident in
their poetry:

The noon sun over Delhi
Lit up the M8....

Yet the country of one's adoption enters the bloodstream, as it were, and
a mind set develops, so one can be jolted by an unexpected spectacle which
records this dilemma of location and dislocation:

Looking over the Lomonds
I saw a llama
On the cooling heights of Shimla
Walking on a cloud of dust.
(Gerry Singh, 'India Gate', in *WIWH*).

Or on seeing

an ambassador
car,

an unlikely
presence,
on Edinburgh
streets....

Many Scots are bilingual yet bilingualism, which should be taken as an asset, often makes a writer feel that she or he is caught in the mire of a no-man's land, existing in a void:

> I've lost something else
> apart from Gaelic and French
> and Canadian English
> choking me in the woods
> leaving me wasted
> in the middle of a family mess
> submerging me here and there
> and out in the Strait
> Nova Scotia horizoned
> And no help in sight...
> (John S. MacPherson, 'One Other Thing', in *WIWH*).

Others who have had to relearn their own language know how history destroys a tongue and can replace it at will:

> Their mouths were like the bells of flowers,
> moist, deep, welcoming,
> and their talk was a fragrance
> which disappeared on the breeze
> when their summer was over
> and they crumpled into dust.
>
> Other mouths will come,
> shapely, shining and winsome...
> and as there is goodness in the soil
> why need I doubt that they will be as sweet?
> (Meg Bateman, 'Language', in *WIWH*).

The fear of losing the heritage of one's language remains a tangible fear.

But writers have learnt the language of their adopted country or the dominant culture. The popular belief that the Calibans of post-colonialism have learnt the language of their masters to curse is the subject of many critical debates. Amidst this on-going dialogue we have Hamid Shami saying:

Yes
I speak
Fluent
Urdu
But
In my dreams
I bawl,
Curse
And swear
In the Queen's
English
('Mother Tongue', in *WIWH*).

There is the reality of the pain of being caught in the dual culture of twin languages as in:

swimming in the clangorous mud
between the roots of my two languages
the one that is red
sprinting swift lightnings through my veins
and the other
                    alien, indifferent, familiar
wrapped around my skin like prison clothes, as I
stretched out the fingers of my reason, my vision
across wavefurrows
to reach all the bays of the world
across broken shellmounds of syllables
to reach the languages of the world

though you should be but
                    across a kyle
a sharp blade lies
                    between our words…
(Aonghas Macneacail, 'The Lost Tower', in *WIWH*).

The struggle to reconcile their two languages continues in present writers:

I'll tell you this—
I'm not Atlas;
I cannot bear the world.
I am only an atom on the surface of the globe,
Struggling between fission and fusion.
It troubles me too
to see a country sink
like a sand-castle beneath the tide,
and a language thrown from us
like a faded paper flag,
and a *Weltanschauung* forgotten
like an empty daydream,
and history disappear without a trace
like a child's footprint on the beach.

I'll tell you this—
I'm not Fionn;
I cannot bear my country.
I am only a cell in Scotland's body,
Struggling to be a brain-cell.
(Fearghas MacFhionnlaigh, 'From The Midge', in *WIWH*).

Yet many writers, with their inherent optimism, can discover bridges to traverse an apparent gap:

Cianalas:
Who would have thought
I'd have to come
So far from home
To find a word that perfectly captures
The voiceless ache
Of having left?

A' dol dhachaigh:
Strange that I should
Find restfulness
In a language where

You can never be home,
But only going
      Homewards.
(Christine Laennec, 'Building Vocabulary', in *WIWH*).

The Scots were travellers because of Britain's maritime colonial past. This part of Scotland's history has not only brought the world closer but also opened the windows of the world onto Britain—and in this case—onto Scotland, so that travel and immigration have become not a dream or a nightmare, but a prospect:

Beyond the flat earth of the boundaries of sense, he knows—
      The world is just a great round ball folk circle to work and live.
A global awareness.
If you spit in the ocean, that drop might reach the nearest shore.
But hoist a sail, and you go where you please, to new found land.
(Robert Alan Jamieson, 'Sea Faring', in *WIWH*).

Though many assume that Britain is a dream country for her post-colonials, immigration has not always been a matter of choice, often entailing uprooting and the creation of a distance between the traveller and her/his much loved birthplace:

A boat, departing slowly over black water
The town, shrinking
I, nothing.
(Suhayl Saadi, 'Slave', in *WIWH*).

Succeeding generations have been born here and drawn into the rhythm of Scottish life, participating in its unfolding pattern. They go to school here and work and play alongside their Scottish compatriots and even represent them. So we see a new Scot participating in a football match, but he is not allowed to forget that he is an outsider:

…Always the odd one out, I was busy
watching the steam spout from my lips
as I walked slowly between the goals

a caesura through the classical mould. Then:
(...Paki-Bastard, Shoe-Shine Boy, Get Back Home:
the mysterious dervish name from Persia
whirled on the thick-set tongue of Ayrshire)....

II

At home, football was just not cricket;
My dad wanted me to bat for India
Or England, depending who was beating Pakistan.
'When in Rome, do as the Romans do'
was his mantra, ...

But with time, the young learn to fit in after a fashion as the poem
concludes:

I peer from a pudding-bowl
As if still batting at the crease;
Waiting for the next bowl
Like an Indian boy
Who knows his place.
(Irfan Merchant, 'National Colours', in *WIWH*).

The poem 'Do' Care' encapsulates this position of a second generation
girl whenever someone tries

To pigeon-hole her Scottishness
And break her brittle brusqueness ...

with questions about her loyalties:

If Scotland played England
Whom would she support
Sco'land—was the answer delivered
And if England played India
India—she claimed with a triumphant swagger
If England played Germany
Germany was the response

From the unassailable position
Of a new-found nationalism.

And what if it were Scotland and India
One demanded with the diabolical confidence
Of an argument-winning lawyer—
She clamped down her glass, shrugged her bare
Shoulders, turned away saying—do' care.
(Bashabi Fraser in *WIWH*)

So the new Scots continue to live here. They marry and finally die here:

... she, for whom we were all assembled,
having come from Yorkshire, long ago,
thrice married in Scotland ...

And how embroidered and sanctified
patterned and interwoven
the lives of Edinburgh are,
divided in liveliness and argument
united in friendship, death and grief.
(Sally Evans, 'Edinburgh Funeral: in memory of Mary Thomas', in *EAIC*).

The movement of people migrating or returning has never been simple. Just as people have arrived in Scotland, there are others who have gone away from familiar places, transforming once lively villages into lonely expanses:

You said a hundred windows shone
a hundred years back in your township
where tonight only your mother's
sends its light over the broken moor.
(Meg Bateman, 'You Said A Hundred Windows Shone', in *WIWH*).

And writers who have moved away from a place they love can be faced with the question as to whether they can return and feel enfolded by an intimacy they once knew in a place they had once been happy in:

...Should I return to live there,
Alone! What community is there? Is it a city for the young or for the
settled
Not for the in-between ...?
(Maureen Sangster, 'Looking for Something I've Lost', in *EAIC*).

With time, the itinerant or trans-cultural writers seek their roots and
realize the pride of having a heritage:

When I looked up, the black man was there,
staring into my face,
as if he had always been there,
as if he and I went a long way back....
'You are an Ibo!' he said, thumping the table....
'The Ibos are small in stature
Not tall like the Yoruba or Hausa.
The Ibos are clever, reliable,
Dependable, faithful, true.
The Ibos should be running Nigeria....
If you went back...
The whole village would come out for you
... fantastic welcome.'
When I looked up, the black man had gone.
Only my own face startled me in the dark train window.
(Jackie Kay, 'Pride', in *WIWH*).

And once they choose to stay, generations blend in with the pattern of
Scottish life and even create their own clan tartan. They thus validate, as
Christine de Luca says, past history, as many had marched to war in Campbell
tartan, and so, today, they can rightfully adopt Scottish tartan in times of
peace, being true citizens of Scotland. And we do know now that of the
65,000 Indians who died in World War II, many were Sikhs.

Edinburgh was a cold host half a century ago
for the tailor from Amritsar; a grey place
for a Sikh who had looked on a golden temple.
There are three generations of Singhs now
to stir warmth into this outpost:

twenty families listed in the phone directory....

The Singh column in the phone directory reveals
New city threads to blend in: a swatch of names,
Of new histories to tartan Edinburgh.
('Blending In: in recognition of 50 years for the Sikh family in Edinburgh',
in *EAIC*).

Many Scottish writers continue living in dual worlds, cultural and/or
linguistic and are, perhaps, the cultural ambassadors of their two countries,
cultures and languages—of one to the other—in a two-way dialogue, as
they stand at the centre like a bridge of tomorrow.

The dual experience of living 'Between ...Two Worlds'—of Scotland
and the 'other' country—is resolved in the poet's acceptance of this inevitable,
unalterable reality, which goes to prove that continents can, indeed, merge
in the imagination of a poet. The experience can sometimes be fraught with
pain, but eventually the poet discovers a positive note in a bridgeable identity:

I came back to Scotland
And longed for the monsoons,
The flocks flying homewards
In the deep sunset glow.
So while the writer can
'experience long daylight'
she can, at the same time
'...pine for the rain'
and remember:

...a country burning
With the sun and my pain
Of living between two worlds
That I cannot maintain,

So while my mother falters
And my father grows old
I hold this my country
As my daughter holds.
(Bashabi Fraser in 'Between Two Worlds', in *WIWH*)

Wolfgang Hilbig

Das
PROVISORIUM

LEIPZIG Hbf

Roman

S. FISCHER

excerpts from *Das Provisorium* *(The Interim)*

Wolfgang Hilbig

translated by Isabel Cole

The Interim is a surrealistic mirror of the author's own experience: it tells the story of an East German writer, C., who in the mid-80s is granted a one-year 'open visa' allowing him to travel freely in and out of West Germany, where he has been given a literary scholarship. These windfalls prove more curse than blessing. At home in neither world, C. succumbs to depression and increasing disorientation. Ultimately he loses all sense of time and place; his odyssey through the two Germanies, in all its grotesque and surreal twists, takes place in an anonymous succession of bars, hotel rooms, shopping malls, strip clubs, trains and train stations. Both Germanies are merely stations in an ongoing nightmare.

(I. C.)

EXCERPT 1

The end of his time in Munich was confused; he had had no hand in it, but played a kind of main role, which made this end perfectly in character for him. Several vivid, almost lurid images lingered, but they loomed in zones of fog, disjointed and nearly impossible to bring into sequence. — Woken by the ringing of the telephone, he had got to his feet, drunk with sleep. If he hadn't had the lightning hope that Hedda was calling, had been trying to reach him all this time, he wouldn't have answered the phone at all. It was dark again already, late afternoon, the rooms were freezing cold. I'm in Munich! he said to himself; each day this was the first thing he thought. And the first thing he felt was a splitting headache, to combat which he always left three or four centimetres of liquor in the bottle. Desperately he searched the three rooms for the telephone, which refused to stop ringing; at last he got his hands on the receiver and answered.

A woman's voice filtered through to his ear, talking much too fast and in endless sentences. It was not Hedda. After a while he grasped that it was meant for him, and that the woman on the phone was the wife of the acquaintance whose apartment this was. —She was afraid he would have to move out... out of the apartment, she meant... today, unfortunately enough, there was no way around it. But of course it was just for the interim...

What? he said.

Just for the interim! Temporarily, just for the holidays, maybe until the beginning of January. Her husband was back from his business trip, had arrived that morning. And he had called over and over again, but no one had answered the phone. Now he was in the car on the way to his apartment... that had been settled, after all, that he would come back on Christmas Eve. She was sorry, she was afraid that this was all rather sudden... rather difficult for him.

C. had only a dim memory of these arrangements for Christmas Eve. — No problem, he said, I'll just pack my things in the meantime.

There really wasn't that much of a hurry. Would he like to come over and have something to eat before they drove to the clinic? Her husband had already spoken to him... or hadn't he? No? Oh, now that was a mess! Well, her husband knew one of the doctors in the clinic quite well, he remembered that, didn't he? And the doctor had agreed to take him on today at short notice, he had to remember something about that! Nothing? But it was all right with him, wasn't it? Of course he'd have to go entirely of his own free will, to the clinic. She was convinced that it was the right thing to do... Hedda would definitely think so too. Her husband had advised the doctor of this alcohol problem, and he had agreed that there was cause for concern.

Have you spoken to Hedda about it?

She thinks it's the right thing to do, you can take my word for it.

What kind of a clinic is it?

A special clinic, one of the best in Munich. At any rate he'd be in good hands there, and he'd be able to rest up. He could stay as long as he wanted.

A clinic for addicts? asked C.

Her husband had looked into all the details, and the doctor, her husband's friend, had assured him that he would be able to leave the ward at any time.

If you say so, I'm sure it's true, said C.; at that moment the doorbell rang, and he hung up the receiver.

Her husband was there, and looked at C.; self-control suffused his features.

Your wife already warned me about you, said C.

Then I'm glad you're still here, his voice was somewhat ironic. The friend took a look around the apartment, and declared: You're already packed! We really had better hurry, after all, it's the twenty-fourth of December.

I've been packed for a month, said C.

You haven't even been here for a month, don't you know that. Still, I'm sorry it had to be the holidays. But that'll mean you'll have some peace and quiet in there.

I don't mind about holidays, said C., I always forget them. Which sanatorium are we going to?

Sanatorium is good! It's called Haar, and it's fairly well-known. Funny name, of course. It's in a very quiet spot outside Munich.

C. remembered having heard the name Haar before. He asked: Is that the insane asylum where the writer Bernward Vesper killed himself?*

Yes... the friend looked surprised. You're well-informed! He was committed to Haar, and he had nothing good to say about it, quite true. The suicide was only after he was transferred to Hamburg. And the clini in Haar has long since been modernised, now it's first-rate...

*Editorial note:
Beruward Vesper was the author of *Die Reise (The Trip)* and partner of Gudrun Ensslin.

In the car, they drove through the night; nothing stirred on the streets of Munich, C. felt that the city was completely deserted. His friend fiddled with the radio, eliciting nothing but the same whining Christmas carols from all the stations; meanwhile C. fell asleep repeatedly in the passenger seat. Waking with a start, he was confused, the ache in the back of his head had receded. Yet it took him a long time to grasp the situation he was in. He felt sobered and defenceless, switched off like the radio, which was silent again now. —It seemed to have got warmer, the wipers swept a grimy deposit of water and snow to the edge of the windshield. Now they were driving along country roads edged by thickets and bare bent trees; the water seen in the headlights, through wisps of fog, trickling from the branches, glistened like a strange organic slime. The area gave C. the creeps, outside the pale of civilisation; there was no oncoming traffic on this road. He felt that they had been driving like this for an impossibly long time, and he hazarded a joke: I feel as if we're about to reach the border...

What border do you mean? asked the friend.

They stopped at a closed barrier which seemed to have appeared out of nowhere; to the right and left of it a strangely harmless-looking fence vanished into the darkness. They were in Haar; outside the friend was negotiating with a gatekeeper; C. thought of grabbing his bag from the back seat and fleeing off to the side into the bushes. As he looked around for the bag, the barrier rose, and the friend took the wheel again. They drove through an agglomeration of buildings which for C. were haphazardly-placed cement blocks; hardly a window was lit. Then they stopped at an entrance next to which a sign with the word Admission could be seen. In an enormous dimly-lit corridor filled with whole parks of leafy evergreen plants, C. was handed over... so it seemed to him. It must have been obvious why he was here, it was announced by his lack of resistance, the helpless way he stood around. His papers were requested, and disappeared a moment later. The friend had asked about the doctor with whom he had supposedly made the arrangements, but was answered only with a shake of the head. C. felt one last stirring of hope that they would send him away again, but suddenly his bag was picked up from the floor, he felt a solicitous pressure on his upper arm; a nurse who must have slipped up unnoticed manoeuvred him to the elevator, whose doors closed before he could say good-bye to his friend. Several floors higher up his bag was returned to him; as C. noticed later, it had been searched.

His friend had been mistaken in the belief that Haar would be especially quiet over the holidays. If anything, the clinic seemed overfilled. Here a perpetual madness was on the simmer, an undercurrent, but ready to explode at any minute, kept down only by the attendants' constant vigilance. C. remembered how empty the city had seemed to him from the car; here, apparently, was the reason. That segment of Munich's humanity which was not presently sitting beneath lit-up Christmas trees had gathered in the asylums for addicts and withdrawal patients to subject itself to a procedure which was called detoxification and which took days, sometimes weeks. Here they were corralled, all those who were not busy now unwrapping consumer goods, those who did not chime in with the thousandth chorus of 'Silent Night', instead striking up a Christmas music quite unlike the conventional kind.

When C. reached his floor, most of the committed already lay in bed, and it was impossible to tell whether they were sleeping or tossing in the throes of their delirium. In the two dim rooms, which were separated only by an open sliding grille and in which there were two empty beds still to choose from, he was met by a stew of sounds whose human origin was not immediately apparent. It was like the suppressed howling and hissing of captive bestial creatures which should not have been shut up in the same room together. More than a dozen men of all ages lay here snoring, yammering to themselves, rattling in their throats. Some of them released a continuous squeezed whimpering sound, as if their chests had been equipped with a peculiar mechanism which went on whistling and squeaking without their volition. All this at once was a song which seemed to come from the nethermost unchristian hells. Others babbled unbroken inextricable sentences that were laments or curses, mad appeals to listeners who were not there; they were 'making speeches', as it was called here. And sometimes this talk swelled, mounted to a bellowing which the neighbours, without actually waking, instantly answered with anxious whimpers.

In such moments a blind shot up with a rattle behind the glass of a semicircular booth which commanded a view of both rooms. The nurse on duty, a stout middle-aged person in a dark-green smock, could be seen looking up from her book and reaching for a bell-button. With the other hand she aimed the beam of her desk lamp outward; swivelling the lampshade, she searched the row of beds for the excited bundle from which the cries emerged. This in itself was enough to reduce the yelling to the level considered tolerable. The beam of the makeshift searchlight swung back to the booth, first moving appraisingly across the other twitching and trembling bodies which, side by side, but without the slightest contact, indulged in their most intimate torments. The cries grew softer and softer, the surges of excitement sank back into the men's bodies; for a while longer they writhed in terror; the blind slid down again.

When day came, C. realised that he hadn't slept a single minute that night. Dried-up he had lain there, and yet drenched with sweat; his body seemed to void moisture through all its pores, he thought he wallowed in the puddles which the synthetic material of the mattress did not absorb. His sweat seemed to mingle with the bitingly sharp and sweetish secretions of all who had occupied this cot before him. After a while he calmed himself and thought, here he had slipped into a kind of circulation which suspended all differences. —Happiness, he thought, does not suspend the differences, on the contrary, it is most solidly grounded on the misery of the subjugated. Misfortune alone obliterates all classifications.

He felt a sudden tranquillity at the thought that he was lying in a bed whose material was saturated with the vital fluids of whole hosts of generations before him. Many had fought for their lives here, had given in, or got away with it one more time... And after him others would come, to live here or to die... he would have been somewhere in their midst, sensing the silken thread on which each hung. It was not necessary to sleep, he thought. He was here to listen to the great noise of torment.

The sleepers in the two rooms had finally grown so weak that they only hummed like heavy sluggish insects. Now came the quiet phase of the night... It is by no means clear, thought C., that there will be life in each of the dark figures on the beds when morning comes. Feeling relatively stable, he got up quietly and began to roam about the rooms. The beds were arranged in two files with as little space between them as possible, so that they could easily be observed from the glass booth, and C. moved as silently as he could. The men lay as if broken by torture, some covered, others almost naked; many wandered open-eyed in sleep or half-sleep, their pupils darting restlessly back and forth. But they did not wake up when C. came to their beds, they stared at him protesting and wild; clearly he was a monster for them, or he took the form of their death. He bent over an old man in concern; from the long thin martyr-figure stretched out on the rumpled bedclothes came an uninterrupted tremor, by turns growing, then fading in intensity. The man was scantily dressed, with ankle-length grey long-johns and a grey cardigan on his naked torso; an undershirt lay under his head.

His mouth foamed as if he had drunk acid, his eyes flickered wildly. And then it seemed to C. that the old man was desperately trying to stammer something out through the choking foam. Was he trying to tell him something? C. bent down closer and thought he heard: Nazis... Nazis... Himmler... Hitler! Thinking he had misheard, C. held his ear still closer to the old man's mouth. Again he thought he heard: Hitler... Himmler... SS... Reichsführer SS!

What's wrong, whispered C., what are you afraid of?

The old man trembled all over, and, with a violent effort, stammered out the word catastrophe.

What catastrophe are you talking about? What could happen...

The man's limbs were shaken so violently that the iron bedstead began to rattle. And his fear instantly infected the sleepers next to him, a general agitation spread. Afraid that the night attendant's blind might snap up again at any moment, C. retreated to his cot.

There were hours in which C. was over-alert, almost hallucinating; he found himself in other spaces that were like enormous train stations filled with people. The people settled on the stone floors of the gigantic halls and tried to sleep; even broad stairways leading into the depths were completely filled. But the stations were all unknown to him. He lay on his bed in Haar and listened to the bridled raging of these men whose sleep was visited by fiends, phantasms, demonic faces. The noise came in waves, after moments of quiet it rose like a distant storm, towered over an invisible horizon and raced forward; under its barrage the bedsteads stamped and jangled, the sleepers clinging tight, each on his own on a whirled-away nutshell, and they joined in, all started yowling at once, but each in his own fear, each picturing his own solitary destruction. Only to slacken again, subsiding as if in a sheltered bay. In the night attendant's booth no notice was taken.

All the floors of the grey cement block were charged with these oscillating waves... and probably, he thought, all the other buildings of the clinic Haar were as well. This was how they kept contact, he thought, with this speechless demonic howling. And somewhere, in this wasteland far outside Munich, the vibrations focussed like electric energies and communed with an equally speechless God.

You remained in Haar until you had spent yourself, until you were burned out, emptied of the rage within you. Then you could go, hollow and extinguished, and dried-up as you were, you would have fill yourself back up with drink one day. Become the dog again who howls to God...

EXCERPT 2

For some unknown time he had experienced the world only in train stations. He moved from station to station, with rare interruptions, his mind retained nothing but the images of train stations, they had become the very points of reference for his consciousness. Nothing in them lent you clear contours, something rapacious was at work in the stations, you were constantly guarding something you hid in your head or your breast: it was nothing of your own, it was sheer egomania. Big-city stations, especially, were the haunt of characters who changed their self-awareness like shadowy clothing; they moved as if they had eyes in the backs of their heads, always in the process of assuming a new appearance, thinking about different destinations, adopting origins which had nothing to do with their own. — In the train stations, C. thought, he was not immediately recognisable as an arrival from the East. That was not the reason, though, for even in the East the train stations had drawn him magically.

Hardly was he reachable at an address in West Germany—first in the town of Hanau—than the circus of author appearances began. From the very beginning the events had struck him as a highly peculiar ritual which went on existing only because no one knew how or why to put an end to it now that they had started. And so these readings went on and on like a bad habit for which there was no longer any occasion. But the fact was that the vast majority of West German writers earned almost their entire living from these readings, with the exception of a few stars, and perhaps the retirees. Wasn't it inevitable that a writer in this country felt like a completely useless figure, reduced to accepting handouts? Or was it just the opposite? Was it the writers' existence as itinerant play-actors which convinced them of being among society's necessary members?

It could be that C. had initially succumbed to a similar delusion. It flattered him when he was invited to large numbers of readings, he accepted all offers assiduously. Later he confined himself to the view that this was how he earned the money he spent... he felt reluctant to use the phrase with the customary shade of meaning: that's how I earn my money.

Few people came to the events: he found it increasingly astonishing that anyone was still interested in literary products at all... and you could count on a good part of the audience consisting of colleagues, that is, of writers who happened not to be on a reading tour themselves. Indeed, most of what was read, what the microphone spouted more or less smoothly into the airspace, whose receptivity was admittedly limited by the size of the auditorium, most of the texts dealt with the conditions of writerly existence. Writers reported on writers, often enough with the more subtle variation in which an author wrote about an author writing about the novelising of a third author... about his difficulties in professional life, or about the circumstances which had led him—or both of them: the narrating author and the narrated author—into the clutches of this profession. In the best cases the subject was a love affair which had come about due to the fact that at least one of the smitten characters was an author; often, both of them were writers.

More than a few texts revolved around the twists of fate which had made the figures into writing figures. Fate was the right word, for the taking of this path was usually described as inevitable. In fact, it was suggested that one was more or less born as a writer. Translated into intelligible speech, this meant nothing but: Provide for me and pay my way—it's not my fault I'm a writer!

This particular phenomenon, thought C., would have curiosity value in other professions. But of course it went along with the very nature of writing, which forced you to appeal to the public... that was the difference from the other professions. A manufacturer of cooking pots appealed to the public too, but only indirectly, he needed them only as buyers for his cooking pots. And if these pots leaked, no matter how pretty they were, no one bought them. For the writer the trouble was that he produced vessels which he had to sell contents and all. Now what happened to him if he found the world full of spoiled contents? It became necessary for the writer to vouch personally for the fact that it was time to look into these spoiled contents... this unquestionably required a certain authority. Could that be the authority of a writer who proffered himself as a touring reader in a completely peripheral culture industry?

C. began to feel more and more leery about the readings to which he was invited. By now he was practically starting to fear them. As the date of an event approached, he vividly felt the dwindling of all power to transform himself in front of the audience into a person who had any respect for himself. He no longer felt any right whatsoever to claim the attention of a group of listeners, however small. The figure which raised its voice there on the little stage had less and less to do with him.

It was a kind of erosion from within, it reached its height the evening before he left for an event; the next morning, when he sat in the train, he slowly began to recover... but how much longer could he keep it up? When he arrived in a city under these circumstances, he repaired to the hotel where he was to spend the night, dropped off his baggage, and then—his first and as a rule only walk through the new city—returned to the train station. The desire to commit this route to memory, for the next day, for the day of departure, did not explain the attraction which train stations had for him. Sometimes, before departing, he passed up one or two trains so that he could linger in the station. The city, its centres, its sights did not interest him, he never truly came to know a city, but he knew the stations, he recognised even those of the most out of the way places, even if it had been a year or two since he had last roamed them. —Once the bookstores had still attracted him, the used book dealers around the station; soon he preferred to stand at the window of a snack bar at the edge of the station hall and look out at the world from within a refuge which was no longer a full part of it, though it was usually found in prominent places around which the city's activity rallied in a semicircle. The activity was closely linked to the train station, but he was already detached from it; in the station he did not stand out with his form of restlessness, on the contrary, here composure reached him, here he need signify nothing but flight and passing-by.

Perhaps most here, in the fastness of the station, were in perpetual search of a pretext to cling to some illusory view of life. Someday they would change their ways, they told themselves constantly, but it was nearly impossible to change your ways in a train station. The arrival and departure halls made a perpetual show of change, and the whole time everything remained the same, you constantly glimpsed in passing the minute in which everything suddenly would have been different. All the things to help you get your bearings, clocks, information from the loudspeakers, electronic departure boards, the perpetual semblance of reliability only brought more powerfully to mind the provisional and fragmentary nature of human existence.

C. tried to picture the train stations in the East, and asked himself whether they had brought similar things to mind. They had sometimes given him the creeps, especially at night, and not only because of the unreliable train service. The stations were more provincial, even in the cities, and they served economic concerns more than the smooth conveyance of passengers. At night, passenger service was relegated to the sidelines, the noisy business of freight traffic dominated the station premises. In general passenger trains ran at longer intervals, but they ran until late in the night... Even past midnight the platforms were dotted with people, tight knots of haggard figures who stormed the compartments as soon as a train pulled in. In no time the grimy ice-cold cars were crammed with passengers, you could count yourself lucky to find a place to stand relatively unmolested in the corridor. When you tried to move through the train you had to pick your way over whole groups of young people who had parked themselves in the corridor with their bags, passing around bottles of schnapps or beer. Often, after swallowing the masses of humanity, the trains would trundle out past the stations and wait... for what? They waited out there in desolate places known to no one, next to lonely dim lamps through whose reddish glow showers of sand, rain or snow sifted, they waited, and time seemed to stand still until some signal gave the go-ahead.

In contrast, the West German train stations seemed more and more to resemble shopping centres, distinguishable from those in the city only in that the closing times were suspended. C. had trouble to keep from getting lost in the train stations the way he always did in the pedestrian zones of the big cities. Without thinking twice he would descend the escalator and arrive in the underground shopping arcades which were found beneath almost all large train stations. Shop came after shop, the drumfire of the neon signs drove the shoppers before them, they were washed up and down the passages by the rhythmic waves of coloured light, and before the Shops and Markets, the Boutiques and Stores, the Cafés and Bars, they were gradually divested of themselves. C. would let the crowd tow him along, panicking intermittently at the thought that he had missed his train. Soon he would be confused and depressed and let the escalator carry him upstairs again.

The trains which carried him out into the country then were almost empty: he was an anachronism, this isolated passenger in his compartment, this book reader in the railway who kept nodding off over the endless pages, waking with a start, shifting his gaze out the window, to the Autobahn, parallel to the tracks, where the herds of cars raced along. It grew dark; resting his head against the window, he watched how they overtook the train. How they bolted forward as if an evil spirit rode their shoulders, giving them the spurs, and they tried to break away, but it would not leave them. How they swept onward, around a curve, and shot toward the railway, how they charged, then struck a course parallel to the tracks, almost standing still for a moment, and then, shifting gears, inexorably pulled away from the train. Disciplined and united in close-massed squadrons, united for one minute, uniform brainless brows behind the windshields, bodies resting death-packed asses on a power which was not their own, fused to a steering wheel which mastered their fists, they fled onward as if set in motion by the lash of a great herd-driver's whip. And this great shepherd was Capital ... he always said to himself when he looked out the windows of the train at the intertwined chains of dimmed headlights, a light-suffused gas-cloud over them, a cloud of sweet Arabian perfumes as of burning pipelines, a cloud of coloured miasmas which drifted along with them as they rushed in formation down the course, gigantic glittering hives of automobiles, and he whipped them on, the shepherd, on from one gas station to the next, where they filled themselves with their manna, tanked up on their divine gas. Stick it to them! cried the shepherd, their God, who had long since grown weary of his flocks.

You stick it! Stick it to them... yes, it was that jaded spirit which hovered over them in the red haze and waved them on faster and faster. You stick it to them! Too lazy for the last rites, he had put all the power into their hands. And when he waved, he waved with their hands. And he raised his sceptre, invisible at the exit of a gas station: Exit! Faster faster! Stick it! Stick it to them! It was the spirit of profit, their shepherd, their God, their great Schicklgruber. And he fired the starting pistol at the glass-smooth exit of every gas station. Aaah! filled with manna they roared off obediently in close formation, and with the joyful cry of death on their lips, and triumphant and with fixed gaze they bore down on the night belt of the Autobahn. Here on the Autobahn, in the intoxication of speed, in the masses, in the toeing of the line between the metal barriers, in the endless tunnel of speed and in artificial light they were aware at last of this blind spot which they all bore within them and which for centuries they had vainly sought to grasp. The empty space in their bodies, the abstraction, here in the midst of the squadron they suddenly knew what it was, this I, this self, it could be translated by a simple foreign word, and its name was none other than automobile. And when the God, the great shepherd, the great Schicklgruber waved his sceptre majestically, motioning out into the open, to the exit, in parting, they followed undaunted their automobile's soul and roared off again: Aaah!

Will we survive this century? asked the lonely reader in his train compartment. Yes, surely we will survive this one last century.

EXCERPT 3

Late in the evening he had walked through Vienna one more time; he lost his sense of direction and suddenly had no idea where his hotel was. — He wanted to drink, that he felt, but not in so-called pleasant company, he did not want to make conversation, accept compliments, take pains to return them, he wanted to drink the way he was used to, speechless, dark and hurried, until something began to live in him, until the beast from the forest which threatened to waste away inside him stirred and stepped forth from his eyes...

He came to a narrow street lit with loud colours, where insistent music blared from the doorways, where the usual swanky affectation of an entertainment district prevailed. Here people were still about, here, mostly in groups, roamed the restless and the addicts whom no global catastrophe could dismay. Meanwhile he had drunk enough, and he managed to walk without hesitation into the first peep show he came to. In front of him the ring- and chain-laden hands of a bearded man with a gleaming bald pate turned the pages of an album in which photos of scantily-dressed girls were filed away wholesale. He tapped one of the pictures at random, without really looking, paid the specified sum and was shown to a booth whose door he shut behind him. He was hardly capable of examining the young woman who performed her show in a set-piece interior behind a pane of glass barely a yard away. She had invited him to sit down, but he remained standing, he even came a little closer to the glass, with a strange sense of duty clear in his mind. He tried to look at her face, but the face revealed nothing but inaccessibility, it existed at a distance which could not be measured in terms of space... while he was still seeking an explanation for this, she, with naturally elegant movements, removed the skimpy pieces of clothing in which she had been dressed when she came in. —He was not here to look at her face, he thought, focussing on her body, on the breasts, on the thighs which smoothly stretched and spread... but suddenly he thought he no longer saw a thing. It was true, he saw nothing, it was as if one of his brain functions had been switched off, he stared between her open thighs and he could see nothing, no, for him she was not visible, this woman, death clutched him by the throat...

He went to the ticket booth, paid the sum again and tapped the same picture in the album which was shown him. This time he had the feeling that a barely-perceptible smile played about the woman's mouth as she appeared behind the glass. The scene repeated itself, she began her mincing movements, undressed; before him, a few centimetres behind a pane of bullet-proof glass, writhed a beautiful woman's body with gleaming skin, and all at once shadows crossed it, miasmas, everything blurred. He felt tears rise into his eyes, he clenched his teeth to get a hold on himself (he had no idea whether she could see him behind her glass), he bit the inside of his cheek until he tasted blood in his mouth, then he left the show.

Outside he leaned against the wall; a cold wind brushed his sweaty forehead, there was a smell of rain. He left the district and came into darker areas, he hardly knew now what he had just experienced. —His senses had failed him, in the crucial moment on which all depended he had been struck with a kind of blindness. The body of a woman offered itself to him, she turned, bent, crouched down, but it had been impossible for him to make out her image; she had reached into her lap and opened her labia, he knew, but he had not seen it...

He found himself near his hotel, more by coincidence, after a bafflingly short walk, and a fine drizzle had started, smelling more of dust than of water. Here, between two side streets, the sidewalk went under arcades, past rows of columns; he went on beneath the arcades... and suddenly he recoiled. He looked at a wall with closed window-shutters, the shutters seemed to have been closed for a long time, their paint was peeling—at first glance the building appeared to be an old theatre which had gone bankrupt—and on these shutters hung posters: with his face!—There were three or four windows at street level, and on all the double wings of the wooden shutters hung posters with his face. With something approaching horror he turned away; he saw that the same posters hung on the pillars behind him... they were the posters for his reading, which had already taken place.

Was it really his face?—It was his face, clearly recognisable, but the fact that it hung here was devoid of all truthfulness. He could not say why it was, but he recognised himself and didn't recognise himself... maybe it wasn't his face after all?—No, this face on the posters had nothing to do with him... only through some inexplicable fatality had he, C., ended up behind this face, which had been photographed in an absurd mix-up and used on the posters for lack of a real likeness of him. The picture on the posters was the picture of a dead man... it was not possible that the past life of this corpse had been his story, his story which lay behind him...

And I must end the story, there is no point to it anymore, he thought. I must put an end to this story at once.

Waterproof

Lars Saabye Christensen

translated by Kenneth C. Steven

Lars Saabye Christensen was born in Oslo in 1953. In the wake of several publishing successes he became a household name in Norway when his novel *Beatles* appeared in 1984. This story of four boys growing up in Oslo at the time of their pop idols, living through the Vietnam years and a whirlwind of revolution and drama, is unforgettable for its tenderness, humour and precise observation of character. It has been translated into numerous European languages, as have several of Christensen's subsequent novels and short story collections. This story comes from *The Jealous Hairdresser*, published by Cappelen in Oslo in 1997. This is the first time Christensen's work has appeared in English.

(K. C. S.)

Each day that whole summer, apart from the week when she was to learn to swim, Andrea stood at the quay and waited as Prince drew in to land. It wasn't the passengers she wanted to see, as they came along the gangway with all their luggage—cases, rucksacks and great parcels from town wrapped in brown paper. It wasn't the Icecream Man who held an interest for her, the man who used fingerless gloves and put on a hat with earflaps each time he opened the freezer that he called his office. Neither was it the Ticket Collector with one thumb on his counter, nor the Captain with the sunglasses he wore no matter the weather that she waited for each and every day.

No, Andrea waited for Buffalo.

Because it was Buffalo who threw the rope. He stood forward on the deck, a couple of steps from the railing, so as to get the throw right, the rope wrapped around his left hand and the knot held in the other. Then he swung it in a bow over his head, or along the line of his shoulders if there was a good deal of wind, then he let go and the rope furled out, circle after circle, bow after bow from Buffalo's left hand, and the knot landed over the bollard that was bolted fast to the edge of the quay.

Buffalo never missed. As Prince glided in slowly towards the fenders Buffalo secured the rope three times, as it tightened and there came almost a song from it, as suddenly it slackened and the drops of water were ranged like a translucent curtain in the clear light between the ship's side and the sky above the fiord.

It was the finest thing Andrea had ever seen.

And when Prince was to turn again and start back once more for town with a new set of passengers, or travel on to Ildjern which was almost at the open sea, and when the Ticket Collector had rung the ship's bell, Buffalo would whip the knot from the bollard with no more than a flick of his wrist, and gather in the rope before it had gone underwater. The knot only skiffed the waves and no more before it vanished over the railing between Buffalo's hands.

Andrea stood there until she could no longer see Prince, the most stylish of all the ferries that plied between the capital and Nesoddland. Sometimes it looked as if the white ship flowed in the air, especially when the sunlight was strong and made everything different, vaguer, dizzy. Then Prince became a swan on the fiord and Andrea had to shield her eyes, and she saw Buffalo roll the rope up and hang it to dry under the ship's deck. After days of rain he would tar it, and then Andrea would be sure she could catch its sharp smell, all the way in to where she stood by the bollard on the quay. Then Buffalo would wipe his white forehead with the back of his hand, light a cigarette, and lean against the railing.

Andrea always raised her own arm in greeting.

And one day Buffalo raised his arm to wave back.

Andrea ran home. The older boys called after her from where they waited their turn by the diving board beyond the red bathing hut. They called her name and dived, they hung in the air like gold inverted commas, landed soundlessly to swim in the backwash of bigger ships.

Andrea pretended she hadn't seen them, that she didn't know them. Their laughter was strange and different. But Buffalo had waved to her. Buffalo had seen her. She ran up the steep slope to the holiday house. It flickered in the midst of the brown heather by the fence, a fire without flames. Her shadow was thin and mysterious in the light of the low sun at her back. She couldn't hear anything, no sound of voices, so perhaps they'd gone for a walk as they did when they were happy. Once she'd seen them hand in hand and she'd almost started to laugh; she stood hidden behind a redcurrant bush and saw them walking hand in hand, but she'd managed to control herself all the same and not laugh. Her father's notebook lay on the balcony, together with his flight timetable, his newly-sharpened pencil and an eraser. Her mother's blue bathing costume was hanging over the wicker chair to dry just as it had hung there for several days now, scorched and pale. Andrea hurried upstairs and let herself into their room. The bed wasn't made; the downie had fallen onto the floor and there was a heavy smell, like that of rotten fish. She went over to the window and lifted down the fire rope from its great hook. It was heavier than she'd imagined. She only just managed to hold it. She thought of Buffalo's arms that were dark brown, almost black. She imagined she saw her parents down by the front door, where the hedge was drowned in a haze of red scent and insects, but it was nothing, nothing at all.

Andrea carried the rope out with her, over to the well behind the house where she wouldn't be seen, into the shadows beneath the birches that criss-crossed the sky in green, moving stripes. There was a tree stump there she could aim at. She put one end through the fastening to make a knot. Then she rolled up the rope as she'd seen Buffalo do and closed her eyes. Now I'm onboard, she thought; now I'm onboard ship and the ship is called Prince— I can feel it rocking, rocking. She opened her eyes, swung the knot as hard as she could, and threw it. It didn't reach far enough—just fell right in front of her feet. She had to hurry to roll it up again for the quay was coming nearer and nearer all the time. She threw a second time and saw that now the knot lay curled around the stump, and she felt herself trembling in the nice way that one sometimes does. She was almost completely carried away with her own triumph and just laughed and laughed. At last she came to her senses and knew what she had to do; she pulled the rope tight and Prince gently came alongside the quay without so much as a bump against the fenders. She counted no more than five passengers who went ashore, and only two came onboard. A moment later she heard the ship's bell and she just gave a flicker of her hand as she'd seen Buffalo do, but the knot remained where it was around the stump. The rope only flickered slightly, like some brown, hairy snake in the grass. She tried once more, harder, more quickly. It was no good. It didn't work. Her hand burned, almost as if she'd held her fingers round a flame. In the end she had to go over to the stump and lift off the knot. She imagined Buffalo's hands that were always dirty, that had to be because of the tar he used after it had rained, and his hands must have smelled just like the rope. She took four steps backwards, turned around, rolled up the rope, swung the knot and threw, opening her left hand so the rope uncurled, and missed. She gathered the rope in again and the waves were stronger now, she could hold her balance just and no more. With the curl of the rope in her left hand and the knot in her right, she threw it, low and quick. This time she did it—almost.

And each evening that summer, apart from the week when she was to learn to swim, Andrea stood at the well, under the birch trees' green light, throwing the rope out in the direction of the old stump.

Then her mother called her from the house; it was supper time. They'd been somewhere for a walk and now they'd come back. Andrea hoped they were still happy. She left the rope there in the grass and ran back to the house. Her mother was in the kitchen, pale despite all the sunshine. The light seemed to go right through her and she cast no shadow. She had a blue-striped apron on and was barefoot. For some reason it made Andrea so happy, the fact that her mother went about without shoes. She looked at her mother's mouth to see if there was a smile there, to see if the lips were turned up rather than down.

Her mother nodded towards the tap.

'Wash your hands before you have supper. And don't use too much water.'

'They're not dirty.'

'Let's see.'

Her mother took both her hands in her own, turned them over and just shook her head.

'Not dirty? Really? Where have you been with those hands?'

Andrea hesitated.

'At the well.'

Her mother sighed, an almost soundless sigh. She could sigh with her eyes too when she rolled them, when the whites of them showed. She let go of Andrea' hands.

'Why aren't you with some of the other youngsters?'

She went to fetch the milk from the fridge. A blast of cold air poured into the room.

Andrea didn't answer. The others? Why should she bother about them?

'Where have you been?' she asked instead.

'Just for a walk.'

Andrea went closer to her.

'Barefoot? Did dad go barefoot too?'

Now her mother smiled at last. Her mouth grew, her face spread wide with smiling.

'No, silly. I took my shoes off when we came home. My feet get so swollen in the heat.'

Andrea looked down at them. She could see that her mother's feet were swollen; they looked like dough, like wet yeast. The toes seemed far too small and the nail of one of them was completely yellow and almost grew right into the flesh. It was ugly.

Her mother stroked her cheek.

'Hurry up now. It's late.'

Andrea took the bread and the milk jug out onto the balcony and sat down with her father. He wrote slowly in his notebook and then rubbed out a wrong calculation, blew away the remains and began again.

He was sunburned. Through his thin hair, when he sat bent over like that, she could see his scalp. It was pale red and uneven, dented, and on his forehead were flakes of dry skin which sometimes loosened and hung in the air, too light to fall.

'Everything's on time so far,' he said.

Then her mother stood there in the entrance to the shadowy living room. She had put her shoes on again. Her mouth was small now.

'Hands,' she said. 'You forgot to wash your hands.'

Andrea hurried into the kitchen, but before she turned the tap she smelled her fingers. The skin smelled dry and tight; she stuck her forefinger quickly into her mouth and licked it. It tasted almost as it smelled, and she thought of tar—tar and sunlight and great circles of hemp.

Then she let the water flow over her hands, the hands she suddenly believed were far too small, that seemed no longer here at all. She heard her mother climb the staircase to the upper floor and close the bedroom door behind her.

When Andrea went out onto the balcony again, her father hushed her before she'd said anything. She hadn't actually been going to make a sound, as if she knew intuitively that she should be quiet. She just sat down as carefully as she could and drank a little milk, but she didn't feel hungry. A wasp hung over the slice of bread that was spread with orange marmalade, its wings almost invisible, a golden point in the middle of an entire summer. She brushed it away with the back of her hand, quite unafraid, and glanced quickly at her father. He was listening. He sat there with his eyes shut and listened. His nose was red too, a red lump in his face. He might almost have been dreaming. But he was awake. He listened, impatient, his eyebrows occasionally rising and falling. Then he smiled, his mouth lifted, he opened his eyes and looked at his watch. Then Andrea heard it too, that noise that swelled and swelled on the other side of the fiord, which spread through the dry haze of that still, blue evening. Then they could see it, the plane that rose up from the runway, almost vertically, and Andrea felt a pull within her head and heart. She saw the passengers and air stewardesses tumbling backwards as the plane rose and rose until at last it finally swung, and for a time one wing shone, bright red, before the plane passed into the thin golden clouds to the south and vanished.

Her father started writing in his notebook.

'Last departure of the day,' he said. 'DC 8 to Copenhagen. Eight minutes late.'

He stuck the pencil in his shirt pocket and looked up.

'That goes for you too, Andrea. Off to bed now.'

'Are you going up yourself now?'

Her father looked the other way.

'I'll stay here for a bit yet. It's such a lovely night.'

A yacht stood still right out in the middle of the fiord. The wind waited.

Andrea went up to her room. She poured some water from the jug into the wash basin, dipped her face into it and laughed, her mouth still underwater. Everything just frothed about her and she leaned her head backwards, breathed out and listened. Nothing, not the slightest sound from her parents' bedroom one wall away, one thin wall away, where her mother slept in silence alone in the double bed. Andrea only heard herself: her hands, her hair, her heart, her tongue. She brushed her teeth quickly, without using too much water. Then she undressed. The warm air flowed softly over her skin. There was no mirror in her room but she could see herself reflected in the window, caught between the light within and the dark without, so thin, so crooked and angular. Andrea was in between, on a thin piece of glass.

She didn't get to sleep before her father had gone to bed. He came upstairs and went into their room. Now her mother too was awake. Andrea could hear them through the thin wall; her father as he pushed his slippers neatly under the bed, her mother as she lit a cigarette and coughed.

'Sometimes I just want to get away from everything,' she said.

His voice was far away.

'Don't talk like that. Please.'

'Don't talk like that. You and your pathetic planes. Don't you understand anything?'

Then all fell quiet. There was no more to be heard. The house lay in silence within its walls. Andrea slept lightly. She dreamed of heaven, of whether one could touch it if one rose high enough and were to lay one's palms against its blue. Of whether it was cold as a skating rink, all strewn with stars, or warm as the ring of a cooker that God had forgotten to switch off. Then she fell into a plane where she was all alone.

All of a sudden her father was there in her room. It was still dark. He leaned over her.

'Have you been playing with the fire rope, Andrea?'

She drew in her feet.

'Yes,' she whispered.

'Where is it?'

'Beside the well.'

He shook his head and went quickly towards the door. He turned round.

'What if the house went on fire? What would we do?'

Andrea shut her eyes. She heard her father walking through the grass. When he came back each step he took was heavy and he breathed deeply. Then all those sounds were gone again, as if nothing at all had happened. Andrea neither slept nor was completely awake; she was somewhere in between, in the same way that she'd seen herself in the window where the light and the dark met. And as she sank towards sleep, ever deeper and deeper, she thought of what her father had said—what if the house went on fire? Tomorrow she would leave the rope by the well again, hidden in the tall bracken behind the stump, and if the fire started on the stairs they wouldn't get out. Her father would run over to the window and find the hook bare, and her mother would shriek and try to trample the flames with her naked, swollen feet.

Andrea woke up, roused by angst and shame.

On one such night she went into her parents' room. They were asleep and their faces were full of peace. They lay there like two strangers, on their respective sides of the bed, in their respective dreams. Were they smiling in their sleep? Or were they just pretending they were asleep? Her mother's fingers were golden. Ash lay scattered about from her bedside table. Andrea put her hand gently on her father's red forehead, and slowly he moved away from it. She saw that the fire rope hung where it was supposed to be on its hook by the window.

On the following day she was back at the quay, early enough to catch sight of Prince away in near the lighthouse in a wave of heat. The boys lay on rock ledges and sunbathed down beneath the bathing hut, their feet in the seaweed. The water dried on their smooth, brown skin until they got up and raced to the diving board and plunged in, one after another, laughing. Andrea sat by the bollard and waited. Her dream was so thin she almost didn't notice it at all. Her shoulders began to burn. She'd got a midge bite just above her knee. She decided she wouldn't scratch it. And suddenly she realized she wanted Buffalo to miss so that she could be the one who put the rope into place. With both hands she would lift the heavy rope that stank of tar and salt, and put it round the bollard, she and no-one else. Andrea hoped that Buffalo's aim would be successful and she wished that he might miss.

She heard someone calling. She thought at first it was one of the boys up on the rocks and had no wish to listen to them. But it wasn't any of the boys. Prince was getting close and Buffalo was standing at the rail calling her. Andrea got up and moved out of the way. Then Buffalo threw out the rope; he swung the knot above his head, let go, and it landed over the bollard. Buffalo didn't miss. He pulled and pulled again on the rope until Prince butted the fenders, the great tyres that hung there, black wheels that expanded soundlessly in the sunlight.

A few people came ashore. Some went onboard. An old lady with a parasol had to be supported by the Ticket Collector. The Icecream Man pulled his hat down over his ears and ate a nut ice. The Captain polished his sunglasses with a white handkerchief.

And Buffalo leaned over the railing, slapped the rope three times and looked at Andrea. She laid her hand quickly on the rope and it shook, she felt the reverberated through her whole body and under her feet.

'Hi,' Buffalo said.

Andrea went still closer, carefully, didn't say anything.

'You're here today as well then?'

Buffalo was smiling.

Andrea nodded.

'Why aren't you off swimming?'

Andrea hesitated.

'I can't swim.'

Buffalo wiped the back of his hand across his forehead as he always did, and his forehead was quite white, unlike the rest of his face that was chestnut, like old leather. It was said that Buffalo had walked bare-legged right across America and back again. He had stayed with Indians and ridden buffaloes along great rivers. All this was boasted of Buffalo, and he had a blue tattoo on each arm and a scar under his left eye that resembled an anchor. Now he put both hands on the railing and they smelled just as she thought they would, but of something else too, of fruit perhaps, soft apples in the September grass.

'What's your name?' Buffalo asked.

'Andrea,' she answered softly.

'Andrea. That's a fine name. Never knew anyone called Andrea before.'

She looked up at him. He wasn't making fun of her. He scratched under his eye as if he wanted to rub out the scar.

The Ticket Collector rang the ship's bell; three short rings followed by three long.

'Don't sit there again,' Buffalo said, pointing at the bollard.

He wasn't annoyed. He'd simply said Don't sit there again. Andrea nodded.

Then he loosened the rope, jerked his hand so that a judder went through it, and drew it in as Prince backed out into the water. Buffalo waved to her until the sun had made him invisible, or perhaps it was Andrea. It was impossible to see where she stood there on Tangen quay in her thin, white dress in the very heart of the light that July of 1964. She kept waving for a while, just to be sure. Then she ran homewards. Buffalo had seen her. Buffalo had spoken to her. Now he knew what she was called. Andrea. She called out her name as she ran. Andrea. I am Andrea.

Her parents had already finished their dinner. Her mother lay asleep on the divan in the living room. There was a pile of cold mackerel left in the kitchen. Andrea ate the cucumber salad instead, with her fingers, without having washed them first. She listened quietly to hear if her mother had woken up over in the shadowy corner of the room. Quiet, everything was quiet, still as gossamer. The milk in the fridge was sour. She drank some water from the tap instead and dried herself with her dress.

Then she sat with her father out on the balcony. He was waiting for the next plane to take off. He wore sunglasses and above his nose there was a piece of paper which he'd torn out of a newspaper. Andrea leant closer. She could make out the cheapest bikinis of the season for only—the rest was gone. She leant back quickly and tried hard not to laugh. Her father stopped writing for a moment, looked at her over his sunglasses.

'What's so funny?'

Andrea shook her head.

'Nothing. Honestly.'

A plane suddenly took off on the other side, a cloud of silver that rose in a great arc and came right over them, then vanished in the clouds to the east and left behind a low thunder. Her father checked the time and wrote in his notebook, his hand trembling slightly.

'The Caravelle to Stockholm,' he said. 'Six minutes early. Amazing.'

He took off his sunglasses and rubbed his eyes. The piece of paper remained where it was for a moment, then dropped onto the table between them. His nose was peeling. His eyes were red. All of a sudden Andrea felt sorry for him.

'Are you going for a walk later?' she asked.

He shrugged his shoulders.

'Don't think so,' he said quietly. 'Your mother isn't feeling too good.'

'Is she ill?'

Now Andrea was whispering herself. Her father scratched his nose.

'No. It's just....'

He fell silent, looked at his fingers, almost as if he'd forgotten what he was going to say.

'What were you doing up there at the well? With the fire rope?'

'Throwing it.'

He looked at her.

'Throwing the rope?'

'Yes, onto the stump.'

'Isn't that a funny game for a girl?'

Andrea said nothing.

'Wouldn't you rather be with some of the others?'

'Amn't I allowed to do it?' Andrea asked quickly.

'Of course, yes. Just so long as you hang the rope up again afterwards. You don't want us to have to jump out of the window if the house goes on fire, do you?'

'It won't go on fire!'

Her father laughed.

'Of course not. I'm only joking…..Quiet!'

Yet another plane took off and flew straight into the sunlight that streamed from the other side of the sky. He wrote in his notebook, in the columns of departure times and types of aircraft: DC 7, London. Andrea looked at his hands that were thin and pale, covered with fine, golden hair. Even his watch was too large for him, hung loose round his wrist.

'Guess how long the flight is from Copenhagen to Teheran?' he asked.

Andrea had no idea.

'Flying with SAS Coronado,' he went on. 'Just guess.'

'Thirty hours?'

'Nine hours and ten minutes.'

Andrea went upstairs and sneaked into her parents' room. The bed was made up now. The room smelled very clean and of tobacco. Her father's brown slippers were lying beside the potty. A half-smoked cigarette lay in the ashtray on her mother's bedside table. The filter was red with lipstick. The window was open and the curtains breathed slightly with a white restlessness. She struggled with the rope and took it out with her to the well. She stood there and threw it over and over again, that heavy knot in that small hand. She had to go closer to the stump and the earth swelled beneath her with great breakers. Almost everyone was already seasick, even the Icecream Man; all of them longed to reach dry land as soon as possible. Andrea kept throwing the rope and finally she did it and the knot encircled the stump, just as on that first day. She pulled for all she was worth and secured the rope tightly round the rusty iron ring on the cover for the well. She waited until all the new passengers had come onboard, then heard footsteps at her back—her mother. She was carrying a bucket and put it down in the grass. Andrea suddenly felt dizzy. She would like to have said that there was no more room, that they couldn't take any more passengers, otherwise the boat would capsize. But she said nothing. Her mother sat on the stump and lit a cigarette. She took a deep drag, closed her eyes, and slowly breathed out smoke, there amidst all that greenness.

Her mother opened her eyes and looked at her.

'Oh, Lord. Your dress is filthy!'

Andrea pretended she hadn't heard. She loosened the rope from the handle. Her mother didn't move from the stump.

'I'm talking to you, Andrea.'

Her name sounded so different when her mother spoke it; heavy, almost like a threat, a stone.

'I can easily wash it myself.'

Her mother sighed and smoke flowed from her mouth.

'What do you do down at the quayside every day?'

'Nothing.'

'Nothing?'

'Look at the boats.'

'All right, Just so long as you're careful.'

Her mother said nothing for a time. A plane rose and disappeared into the southern skies. She stubbed out the cigarette under her shoe.

'I may go into town before you two.'

Andrea turned to face her.

'Don't sit there again,' she said.

Her mother laughed abruptly. She suddenly looked stupid.

'What?'

'Don't sit there again.'

She got up slowly from the stump. The two of them stood there, just a few feet from each other, in silence. Andrea held the rope with both hands. Soon it would be dark. A cloud drifted through the branches of the birches. The bracken rustled. They could hear the fiord; the waves against the seaweed, the sound of their backwash.

At last Andrea's mother lifted the bucket that lay on its side in the grass.

'Will you give me a hand, Andrea?'

Her mother went over to the well. Andrea hesitated a moment, then hurried after her. They shoved to one side the ancient wooden cover that was crawling with spiders and black, glistening beetles. Andrea leaned over the well mouth, stared down into its deep, almost green, shaft. The water level was low; she could just make out her reflection. Her mother wound down the bucket, whipped it round, and when it was full they hauled it up between them. Andrea felt a sinking in her stomach as they pulled the bucket up; she leaned so far over she could have fallen in now... She could have fallen in at any moment, down through the narrow shaft with its spiders and beetles, and nobody would have heard her when she landed. Together they pushed the lid back into place. Andrea felt cold.

'Shall I carry the bucket?' she asked.

'Take the fire rope instead.'

Andrea pulled it behind her through the grass. Her mother walked a couple of paces in front of her, didn't spill so much as a drop from the bucket.

'Don't use so much water from the tap,' she said. 'We must try to save.'

Andrea caught up with her.

'Why are you leaving before us?'

Her mother stopped and picked up the bucket with her other hand.

'I've just something to sort out. We can talk about it some other time.'

Andrea's father appeared on the doorstep by the kitchen. He gazed up at them, smoothed back his thin hair. Then he slowly turned and went inside again.

That night Andrea dreamed that there was no water left in the well. When she let down the bucket there was just a hollow dunt, over and over again, and the spring dribbled slime and rust whenever she went to drink from it. Afterwards she dreamed that the fiord had gone dry and that Prince ran aground beyond the point and capsized among seaweed and empty shells.

She was awakened by the rain. The rain had come. She got up and ran over to the window. There was rain as far as her eyes could range, so heavy that the heather and the grass were afloat, and each and every leaf a green tongue in the downpour. Now she could wash her dress. Now she could drink just as much as she wanted. She got dressed quickly and went downstairs. There was nobody there. The living room table was set, the breakfast things hadn't been cleared away. There was eggshell on the blue cloth. A crumpled napkin. She took a mouthful of cold coffee from her mother's cup but couldn't bring herself to swallow it. There was a newspaper on the floor. Had she slept in? Was it already late in the day? It didn't matter as long as she still got to Prince in time. Maybe she could borrow an umbrella from her father, a big black gentleman's umbrella? The sun was boring. Rain was magic. Rain was freedom. She could do what she liked. She could go through the rain till her dress was clean. But as she was about to hurry off out, her mother suddenly appeared in the doorway, blocking the way out onto the balcony.

'Where are you going?'

Andrea stopped and looked at her. She wasn't wet. She must have been standing there the whole time under the awning.

'Down to the quay.'

Her mother smiled and came closer.

'Have you forgotten, Andrea?'

Andrea was suddenly frightened. She began backing away.

'What?' she whispered.

Now her father stood there too. His face was full of rain and his hair ran down in rats' tails from his head. Her mother turned towards him and gave a laugh.

'She's forgotten. And she was looking forward to it so much.'

Her father was shaking the rain from himself.

'You'd better remind her then.'

Her mother squatted in front of her, put her hands on her shoulders.

'You're going to learn to swim. The class begins today.'

Andrea stared past her mother. Her father was drying his face with a handkerchief.

'It's raining,' she said.

'That makes no difference. Go and get your costume.'

'It's raining,' she repeated.

Her mother's mouth showed that impatient curl and there was a sigh in her eyes.

'You'll get wet anyway, won't you? And you can borrow my big towel.'

Andrea bowed her head.

'I don't want to,' she whispered.

'Don't want to? You'll be the only one who can't swim. D'you want that?'

Andrea closed her eyes. She wouldn't be there to meet Prince. Now Buffalo would have to throw the rope on his own. What if he missed?

'I can't,' she said.

'Can't? What d'you mean, you can't?'

'I've just had breakfast.'

'You jolly well have not. Now come on, we're going.'

Her mother carried the big bag with her swimming costume, her swimming belt, the thermos and the large towel. Her father walked alongside holding the umbrella over them, getting just as wet as before. He wanted to come too even though he never went to the beach—Andrea couldn't remember him swimming a single time. Her mother walked with her arm in arm, as if she was scared Andrea might run off.

'Next year you'll be able to get your swimming badge,' she said. 'Just think of that!'

The others were there already. They stood shivering by the water's edge, all shrunk into themselves, four girls and one boy huddled together, frozen blue shadows between the rain and the sea.

Then Andrea saw Prince glide past out there beyond all the rain. Buffalo leaned against the railing; he was wearing a green sou'wester and he couldn't see her, of course. He didn't see her because he couldn't know she was there. Andrea was about to wave to him but changed her mind at the last moment, put her hand behind her back instead.

Her mother smiled down at her.

'D'you know any of them?'

Andrea shook her head. Prince disappeared round the side of the islet.

She had to change in the bathing hut. She took off her clothes slowly. There were names and hearts and arrows carved into the walls, and some of the words she only dared say in her head before she had to turn away, not wanting to look at any more. It smelled horrible in there, as it did in her parents' room when they hadn't aired it properly, or in the outdoor loo at night. On the floor lay an empty cigarette packet and a flattened beer top. Someone had left a diving mask behind. There was a crack in the glass; perhaps someone hadn't wanted it any more and had just chucked it in there. Andrea drew the mask over her face and sat down over in the corner. She heard the shrill sound of a whistle; it sounded terribly far away.

The door opened. It was her mother.

'Are you coming?'

Andrea looked at her through the cracked visor. Her mother was a thin, lop-sided fish on the sea bed, her tall fin erect outside the cabin of a sunken galleon.

'Oh, Lord, what on earth are you doing?'

'I can't get my swimming belt on.'

Her mother dragged her onto her feet, ripped off the diving mask and pulled the swimming belt tightly round her. Andrea felt the knot of it against her back, digging into her skin like a drawing pin.

She went down to the edge of the beach and stood at the very end of the line. Andrea was the oldest. They all glanced quickly at one another and tried to smile, with blue lips that had forgotten how to talk, that seemed to have disappeared into their mouths. All the parents stood on the jetty close by with thick jumpers, rainwear, gloves, boots and umbrellas. They smoked and drank coffee out of big mugs, and called out encouragingly, clapped and laughed. The peripatetic swimming instructor wore a yellow training suit that was visible under his see-through raincoat. From his neck there hung a whistle and in one hand he held a boat-hook. Then he shoved them forward, one after the other, and Andrea felt the hook on her shoulders as they had to wade out into the water. The cold rose within her like an electric shock from feet to forehead. She could hear the instructor's hoarse voice: In, get right in, you sissies, and all the laughter of the parents. Andrea lay on her front in the cold, grey water, and a wave hit her smack in the face. For a moment she couldn't breathe and she flailed her arms about and kicked with her legs before realizing the water was still shallow, that it barely reached her knees. The swimming belt was heavy and clammy against her body, and the knot burned into her back.

The swimming instructor squatted in the water and shouted through the rain:

'Deeper in! You're not in your bath at home!'

He poked Andrea onto her front with the boat-hook and pushed her towards the waves out past the diving board. Andrea closed her eyes and floated on her side, like a helpless bird. She imagined she heard an engine deep down in the water and she listened to it; its sound was strangely beautiful. She wanted to go further out still now, where they wouldn't be able to reach her. She tried to push out with her feet and make an arrow of her hands. Then she felt the boat-hook again, its tug under the cord of the swimming belt, and she was dragged ashore. On dry land her mother bundled her into the towel and the other five were wrapped up in ones equally huge; five white faces that shook, that looked at each other again for just a moment as their mothers dried them so hard it hurt. Their fathers stood with their backs to them, smoking in the rain; they paid the swimming instructor for six lessons and he counted the money over and over again.

That was the way the days went that week, the week Andrea wasn't on the quay when Prince docked. It kept on raining; the swimming belt got heavier, the knot tighter and tighter, and the water felt colder than ever.

The boy was the first to give up. No-one said a word as he crawled ashore, got his things and went off, his swimming belt in his hand. He walked hunched, his neck white, thinner than glass, all alone. Their parents had lost interest in the end and stopped coming; they had other things to do, and soon it was just the peripatetic swimming instructor who was left standing on the jetty. He grew impatient and bad-tempered; he barked at them, smoked an ever-increasing stream of cigarettes and dunted them so violently with the boat-hook that they all but went under. When Andrea went to bed at night she had bruises on her skin and a deep dent from the knot of the swimming belt in the small of her back, just where it was almost impossible to reach with her hand.

On the final day the swimming instructor climbed down from the jetty, took off his shoes and socks, turned up the legs of his training pants and jumped into the water, using the boat-hook as a support.

'Right, off with your swimming belts!' he shouted. 'Now for the real thing!'

They had to help each other undo the knots. It was still raining; it had never stopped and their fingers were soft and white and wrinkled, like blotting paper. They fumbled and shivered as they stood there, all but naked, and then the instructor blew his whistle and they jumped, one after another, out into the hard water, and they floated, they floated after all. Andrea managed four strokes, then she had to let her feet sink again to the bottom and she pretended to swim as she just tiptoed over the shore between shells, seaweed and stones. One final time she felt the boat-hook dunting her, dragging her, bruising her.

'Get your legs up, you little cheat! You don't fool me!'

Andrea stood up instead and waded past him. He tried to stop her, but she shoved the boat-hook back at him and he lost his balance, fell backwards with a great splash. Andrea got her clothes and towel and went up to the house without looking round a single time.

Her father was sitting on the balcony in his waterproofs. The wicker chair was empty and her mother's swimming costume was gone. Andrea waited. Her father looked down at his notes; the lined pages were all blotted.

'Lots of delays,' he whispered. 'It's the weather, of course. Difficult conditions.'

'Where's mum?'

'In her room. Don't disturb her.'

Her father sharpened his pencil until it broke. Then he started all over again.

'Do we have any tar?' Andrea asked.

'Tar? In the shed, maybe.'

He looked at her for a moment and a smile spread across his face.

'Have you learned to swim then?'

She nodded.

'Good.'

He bent over his notebook again as the sound of a plane sank through the clouds. Andrea hung her swimming belt over the wicker chair and went upstairs, stopped outside her parents' room. She heard footsteps going back and forth across the floor. She bent down and peeked through the keyhole. Her mother was packing a case. She smoothed a green dress and carefully put it in. She fetched three pairs of shoes, put them in small bags, and placed them on top. Finally she stuffed her faded bathing costume into a corner of the case, but immediately changed her mind and brought it out again, shoved it into the wastepaper basket by the basin. She took a quick drag from the cigarette that lay in the ashtray, pressed down the cover of the suitcase and clicked it shut. Then she sat down on the bed to finish her cigarette.

Andrea didn't dare go in, she didn't dare fetch the fire rope. She could tar it tomorrow; tomorrow she could do it after she'd been to see Buffalo. Instead Andrea went to lie down, even though it was still early, about mid-day or thereabouts. If they came and asked why she was lying down she would say that she was ill, that she'd got fever from standing a whole week in that cold water. She could say she had a sore back, and she only had to show them all the bruises from the boat-hook. But no-one came at all. She could hear nothing but the rain, the neverending rain against the roof and on the window and in the trees. Then she went to sleep nonetheless.

She woke up because she'd been sitting up in bed. She'd said the words aloud, the words she'd read in the bathing hut, the words the boys had carved into the walls with a knife or perhaps with a piece of glass. She hid her face in the downie; had anyone heard her? Everything was still—it wasn't raining. She pushed back the downie. Perhaps she'd only said them inside her head, those other words? Suddenly she saw that there was a parcel lying on her bedside table. She tore off the paper and found a small box inside. Inside the box was a watch. A Certina, with a red, braided nylon strap.

There were letters engraved on the square clock face and Andrea read them, one after the other, individually—waterproof. She didn't understand what the letters made up, nor did she know why she'd been given a present. It was just an ordinary day, the third of August, 1964, and the time was twelve minutes past ten.

She fastened the watch and ran downstairs. Her father wasn't on the patio; only his notebook lay there, its pages sodden and illegible. She couldn't hear her mother anywhere either. Andrea called softly but no-one appeared, no-one answered. She waited for a time. The air was cold and clear; she could count the needles on the pine tree by the flagpole. A jagged edge of breeze blackened the fiord, making the waves choppy. Then she couldn't wait another moment. It was twenty-five to eleven. She put on an old jacket, buttoned it all the way up, and went off down to the quayside. She had no need to run now that she had a watch.

And Andrea saw Buffalo on deck, the rope in his hand, as Prince glided in towards the quay. Buffalo threw the rope, and the heavy smell of tar spread through the air, and Buffalo didn't miss. Andrea went over towards him as he was tying up. The rope creaked. Buffalo looked up. He was wearing a scarf and gloves.

'Hi, Andrea. Where have you been then?'

He hadn't forgotten her.

'Swimming lessons.'

More passengers went onboard then came ashore. Soon it would be autumn. The Icecream Man stood with his back to them.

'Why do you tar the rope?' Andrea asked.

'So that it won't fall to bits,' Buffalo answered.

The Ticket Collector rang the ship's bell.

Buffalo looked at her again.

'So did you learn to swim?'

'Almost.'

Buffalo laughed and loosened the rope.

'Either you can swim, Andrea. Or else you can't.'

Once more the rope danced as the knot rose from the bollard and Buffalo drew it in and up over the side. Prince backed out into the water and Buffalo waved. She waved back, but something made her turn round, perhaps because the Ticket Collector had opened up the little gate to the gangway again. Andrea turned round and heard her the same instant she saw her; her mother coming down the road, trying to run, the case banging against her hip as she waved with the other arm and called out. Andrea saw everything; her mother trying to reach the boat, the empty diving board, Buffalo rolling up the rope as each circle became smaller and smaller. She saw Prince turn, heard her mother's calling and the laughter that came from the bathing hut. Andrea ran to the shelter on the quay and hid there, squatted behind the mailboxes. Her mother hadn't seen her. Now her mother had stopped right at the edge of the quay; she'd put down her case and was standing there getting her breath back. She had sunglasses on. It was four minutes past eleven. Everything was made ready for docking. Buffalo raised his arm and took aim, but for a second he hesitated because he looked at Andrea instead of at the bollard, and when he threw the rope he let go too soon and missed. Andrea got up, hesitated, but had already made up her mind, and what followed no-one quite dares say exactly, for all of it happened so fast. The Ticket Collector maintained that Buffalo tripped on the rope, and the Captain reckoned he just slipped, for the deck was wet after a whole week's rain. The Icecream man has still not said a word.

At any rate Andrea leapt forward to put the knot in place. She had to sort things out because Buffalo had missed. Her mother turned towards her in astonishment and cried out before anything had even happened. As Andrea bent down to lift the rope, Buffalo pulled it towards him, and Andrea didn't let go because she was going to fasten the knot herself. She was pulled with it and fell into the sea, down into the black swirling foam beneath the fenders and the ferry.

They dragged the fiord for Andrea for five days. Buffalo went onto dry land for good and he carries a rope with him across beaches and over rocks. Shutters are nailed over the windows of the holiday house. A suitcase stands on Tangen quay, and somewhere, deep in the fiord, time keeps on going.

Reviews

Alasdair Gray — Smollett and Scott — children's plays — Crichton Smith — Jessie Kesson — Anne Carson — poetry

Edinburgh Review seeks to publish an eclectic selection of reviews covering small small press material, books of Scottish interest and works of contemporary philosophical, political and cultural thought. Please send books for review for the attention of the Review Editors, Edinburgh Review, 22a Buccleuch Place, Edinburgh, EH8 9LN

Stephen Bernstein — *Alasdair Gray*
Bucknell University Press hbk
£27.50
ISBN 0-8387-5414-7

Despite Alasdair Gray's national and international significance, his work has not yet received the attention possible in a book-length monograph. Bernstein's work comes forward to fill this gap. One anticipates a thesis which will somehow go beyond the scattered interpretations which can be found in the many articles which have been devoted to Gray. In particular, the rather disappointing quality of much of Gray's later work means that this expectation is particularly keenly felt with regard to an understanding of his superior early fiction.

Unfortunately, the most disappointing aspect of Bernstein's work is his analysis of *Lanark* and *1982 Janine*. His discussion would, in both cases, be perfectly worthy of a journal article. However, in a book entitled *Alasdair Gray*, something rather more profound and comprehensive should be expected from an analysis of Gray's two most important works. As things stand, however, Bernstein develops an interesting reading of the cartographical metaphors in *Lanark*, and a capable, if not particularly original, overview of *1982 Janine*. Bernstein himself remarks that because of the 'voluminous attention' received by *Lanark*, he has felt free to pursue a 'narrow but [...] important and revealing reading'. To this, one can only respond that, as the 'Critic' in Lanark remarks, 'to have an objection anticipated is no reason for failing to raise it.'

Bernstein's monograph starts to come alive, though, in his discussion of Gray's later work. He is cheerfully dismissive of *Something Leather* as a 'set of chapters that only marginally resemble a novel'. He is also critical of Gray's tendency to rehash dramatic work into prose fiction, and to thereby run the risk of 'scene after static scene of dialogue.' Bernstein's favourable readings of *Poor Things* and *A History Maker* also become more informative and synthetic. He is particularly interesting and challenging in his discussion of the Utopian visions to be found in both these novels. Critics will find, for example, much food for thought in his argument that, in *A History Maker*, 'the production of history [...] becomes a clear necessity [...] to the men'. This is the kind of thesis that could productively be examined against all Gray's output, and would have proved, I believe, an excellent focus for Bernstein's own monograph.

Bernstein, furthermore, has a good eye for detail, and this profitably informs all his readings. He notes, for example, that *1982 Janine* ends on the 'morning of 26 March 1982' when 'Great Britain was abuzz with the news that Roy Jenkins of the Social Democratic Party [...] had won the previous day's Glasgow Hillhead parliamentary by-election.' Bernstein is particularly acute to understand this 'conjunction of Jenkins's and McLeish's victories' as a hint of burgeoning Scottish autonomy in the gloomy Thatcher-Major years. The rest of Bernstein's book shows a similar attention to the particulars of historical context, intertextual allusions, and all the other nitty-gritty of close-reading. Only in the connection of this detail does Bernstein tend to stumble; he never quite achieves a comprehensive synthesis of the various readings provided in each chapter.

Despite this failing, *Alasdair Gray* is surely a worthy addition to the growing corpus of criticism of Gray's work. It will, I believe, prove particularly valuable in its attempt to overcome what Bernstein refers to as the 'trans-Atlantic diminution' of Gray's reputation. A voice like Bernstein's is vital if a geographically peripheral author like Gray (as well as the Scottish critical corpus which examines him) is to be properly received in the USA. Certainly, this book will not prove to be the classic and comprehensive examination of Gray's work. However, one can only be critical to a point: an American scholar and an American university press have together produced the monograph on Gray which has been conspicuously absent from the output of Scottish academic publishing.

Gavin Miller

Robert P Irvine —
Enlightenment and Romance: Gender and Agency in Smollett and Scott
Peter Lang pbk £24.00
ISBN 3-906758-5091-X

Critical material on Walter Scott often seems stuck somewhere between Georg Lukacs and Northrop Frye. Is Scott the inventor of the historical novel or the paradigmatic romance writer? These alternatives are multiplied by the positions open to the critic: is Scott to be read within his historical context, or does his work make more sense considered in terms of atemporal archetypes?

There have, of course, been many sophisticated attempts to avoid having to choose between these positions, and to develop an account of Scott's authorship in which all these possibilities are taken into consideration. It is with these attempts that Robert Irvine's book belongs.

Irvine situates Scott's work against the rise of the discourses of the human sciences in the eighteenth century, specifically the threat to agency implied by their deterministic account of history in which society, rather than the individual, is the most significant category. The authorial techniques of the female writers, who dominated the literary market-place when *Waverley* was first published, had developed to figure a space for feminine agency. By adapting these techniques to the novel in general, Scott's books act out a recovery of agency in general. Yet the cost of this recovery is of course the retreat into romance.

Irvine is effectively arguing out a crucial wrinkle in Ian Duncan's *Modern Romance and Transformations of the Gothic*. Both adapt the work of Frederic Jameson to understand the development of the novel in this period. Where Frye understood genres, and romance in particular, as timeless narrative essences, Jameson demands that they be historicised, and understood as the product of a particular set of social and economic conditions. Irvine and Duncan both account for Scott's use of romance forms in these terms.

Yet what Duncan leaves out,

according to Irvine, is the central role of gender. In detailed readings of *Guy Mannering* and of *Rob Roy*, as well as discussions of *The Heart of Midlothian* and *Redgauntlet*, Irvine demonstrates convincingly that gender plays a key role. At a crucial point in the book, this is turned back against Frye and Jameson: 'the subsumption of agency by plot, while fulfilling a compensatory or redemptive function in the face of history [...] also involves an effacement of another sort of agency.' This second form of agency can be read as 'a genuine resistance, however compromised or limited, to a discourse of historical determin-ation.'

Irvine proceeds to argue, and here his work is reminiscent of Cairns Craig's work on nineteenth century Scottish fiction in *Out of History*, that the *Waverley* novels open up the possibility of a prose form which absorbs and relativises the discourse of the human sciences, by juxtaposing them with the full range of narrative and generic forms which Scott's books display. Specifically, and this is Irvine's important contribut-ion, the power to do this is associated with women.

To pick one example, it would be possible to claim that Diana Vernon is the real heroine of Irvine's book. What Diana's 'eloquence' includes is an ability to 'turn her gaze on the discursive practices in which her own identity is constructed.' Frank, Irvine points out, is 'silenced and confounded' by Diana, in Scott's text. However the agency ascribed to Diana can only be dreamt of by Frank, and by Scott, who are doubly alienated from the discourse of history, and the extra- or anti-historical force of feminine oral loquacity.

Smollett's role in the account is as a key transitional figure in the development of the novel in the period, and as a model for Scott. As in Irvine's readings of Scott, so his chapter on Smollett is full of detailed accounts of the social and discursive context of the writing, enabling us to make the requisite connections between the texts and their times.

I am unable to challenge Irvine's reading of the texts at any point. However, there is a difficulty with his account, but one which is entirely beyond his control, and of which he must surely have been aware when writing the book. The changes in the available frameworks for understanding the world against which Irvine sets his suggestive history of the novel, are precisely those that generate the possibility of the kind of account he gives. The distinction between romance and historical narrative which Scott both presumes and then has to negotiate in his novels, is itself a product of the rise of a deterministic historical account.

Irvine, in his turn, can only repeat this distinction. At the heart of his book there remains a tension between romance and realism, between myth and history, between ideology and critique—a debate that has always hinged on the claim to be able to tell the two respective narratives apart. If this is not, in fact, possible, but the product of certain kinds of judgements, and of reading protocols, it becomes rather unclear whether Irvine is not simply repeating the romantic recovery of narrative and agency against history. Which would mean that he, in his turn, must adopt and repossess the authorial position of the eighteenth century female writer, while Scott is cast as the romance hero whose actions are dictated by events beyond his control. In other words, wouldn't Irvine himself be positioned alongside Scott as another of Diana Vernon's admirers, 'silenced and confounded' by a female loquacity to which he has no access?

Alex Thomson

Stuart Paterson
— *Cinderella*
Nick Hern Books pbk £7.99
ISBN 1-85459-484-2

— *Hansel and Gretel*
Nick Hern Books pbk £7.99
ISBN 1-85459-483-4

In these two plays for children, published to coincide with new productions at the Royal Lyceum and Dundee Rep, Stuart Paterson has moved away from the pantomime genre to try and regain something of the power of the original stories. Folk and fairy stories have a special quality that comes from taking common experiences and translating them into metaphor, reflecting something of the human psyche; we feel as if they have, in Paterson's words, 'crawled out of the swamp with us'. The writer tells in the afterword to these two plays how, when he heard *Hansel and Gretel* for the first time, he felt 'as if someone had spied on his dreams', so strong was the recognition of the feeling of abandonment in the story. It is this insightful quality that Paterson tries to recreate.

Paterson's use of the folk tale formula is obvious when these plays are read together as they follow a similar structure—wicked step-mother sends unwanted child/children in to danger out of which

they must emerge stronger and wiser. The characters the heroes meet—the magical assistant, the evil force, the father figure, the helpers who hold the keys to escape—are archetypes recognisable from folk tale studies. The plays are following a basic 'rites of passage' pattern which has been employed by storytellers for thousands of years to pass on wisdom to the next generation. For children the stories can guide them through the minefield of growing up—as adults we can remember and identify.

Despite his obvious respect for the folk tale genre, Paterson has not been afraid to alter the stories. To create an affirming narrative Paterson needs a stronger Cinderella than one readily wooed by wealth and power, and equally his Gretel must use more than an easy, violent solution to her problem. These reworkings do raise questions, as it seems there has to be a reason why we have found these stories with their original endings so compelling for so long. Surely whatever it is in our psyche that allow them to be this way is worth exploring instead of taking what could be construed as the easy option of alteration? Paterson selects images that suit his purposes, but Stepmothers for example may wonder why they have not been spared in his editing.

Paterson has also employed

imagery and metaphor to emphasise the power of these stories. His language is simple, and accessible to a young child's ear, but it resonates with a poeticism that lifts it out of the realms of simple story telling. Moments such as when Gretel asks, falling asleep, 'Can you feel the moonbeam, Hansel? Pulling us up and up, into the wind and out again', are deeply emotive in a way that is never seen in more traditional pantomime. Another move away from panto is the lack of any Scots language or colloquialisms, which together with the lack of any reference to contemporary culture sets these plays outwith our world. Local dialect does make panto feel like a community affair and this accessibility is missing from these plays; however, this does result in the metaphorical aspects of the stories becoming more significant. For example, the image of the white bird in *Hansel and Gretel* as representative of their mother's love leading them into and out of the dangerous wood is particularly well constructed and employed.

Although Paterson is looking to create a 'more genuine and powerful form of dramatic story telling', he is a wise enough dramatist to include elements that ensure panto's continuing popularity. Slapstick humour runs throughout, along with touches of grotesque anarchy such as Cinderella's sisters eating a cake laced with dog pee. Opportunities for audience participation are included and body parts well represented, although the Fairy Prince turned monkey in *Hansel and Gretel* bears more resemblance to the Prince trapped in a swan's body found in folk tales than to the dancing pantomime cow.

Paterson has taken elements of panto and of older styles of story-telling to create work that is engaging and entertaining. Roll on Christmas and another chance to see these great plays performed. Until then, read and relive.

Alison Reeves

Iain Crichton Smith —
A Country for Old Men and
My Canadian Uncle
Carcanet Press pbk £7.95
ISBN 1-85754-474-9

For Iain Crichton Smith, unlike Yeats, the passage of time did not alienate from the country that inspired. Rather than lamenting the effects of time upon his country he revels in the very minutiae of his everyday existence there, both past and present. From the memory of 'the leaking toilets of his primary school' to the immediacy of 'the leaves [that] are turning brown',

Crichton Smith wades backwards and sideways in time, delving into the past through the freshness of the land, and setting up a psychic conflict that runs through the collection. The ageing body with its 'flaking skin' is juxtaposed with the raw emotions evoked in 'nightmares/ of the friends he betrayed' as nature infiltrates the 'unprotected' mind, drawing away from the grim reality of bodily frailty. This poignant conflict of memory and body, however, is constantly interspersed with 'shorts' that shock the reader back to the here and now. Irreverent, sometimes obscure, these snatches of verse span subject matter from fame to love to fences, and appear as flashes of the present in a battle with the past.

By dealing with the simplicity of quotidian experience, Crichton Smith has captured the phantasms of memory that occur in our daily geographical surroundings:

Do you remember
Chapel Street and Summer
Street? We are ghosts.
Past selves remain obstinately in the frosts
Of Aberdeen and Lewis

But he fights morbidity, opting instead for a sense of resignation that belies the complexity of the underlying issues of alienation and exile arising from the encroachment of colonisers on the land and time upon the body. Instead of anger at the enforcement of the English language over his native Gaelic, he speaks simply of its elemental value —'the language of the sea'—that has shaped him prior to the imposition of Anglicised systems.

The second part of this collection, *My Canadian Uncle*, is an extended narrative poem that explores the issues of exile from an observer's perspective. The distance of the narrative voice allows it free play in space and time, criss-crossing the voice of the speaker and his uncle, as geographical exile intertwines with a deeper rooted sense of temporal alienation: 'I don't know/ I tell you, anyone in Lewis now.' The inescapable effect of time upon an individual's relationship with a place runs through the whole collection, as unity gradually becomes achieved only by bringing the past into the present. Indeed, this final collection is in itself an act of remembrance, sent to Crichton Smith's publishers before his death accompanied by the words 'I am sending you this in case anything should happen.' *A Country for Old Men and My Canadian Uncle* look to confront serious issues of exile and separation by concentrating upon the seemingly insignificant and random events that make up everyday life. With a graceful simplicity these poems trace the memories that emerge from the mundane and explore the deep-set difficulties that undercut even the arbitrary aspects of day-to-day existence.

Katy Mahood

Jessie Kesson
— *Where the Apple Ripens*
B&W Publishing pbk, £5.99
ISBN 1-903265-00-2

— *Somewhere Beyond*
B&W Publishing pbk, £5.99
ISBN 1-903265-01-0

In an interview with Isobel Murray in 1985, Jessie Kesson identified the focus of her work: 'But I realised myself what I was writing aboot. At long last... And I thocht, that's it, that's really what everything I've written is aboot – queer fowk! Queer fowk, who are oot, an niver hiv ony desire to be in!... Every work I've ever written contains ae ootlin. Lovely Aberdeenshire word. Somebody that never really fitted into the thing.'

'Ootlins' are exactly what Kesson writes about in the eponymous novella in *Where the Apple Ripens* and the other ten short stories contained

in this wonderful collection. In essence, Kesson's work is about characters, as she recreates and celebrates the 'queer fowk' of rural Aberdeenshire where she grew up. The regionality of these stories maps out the topography of the countryside of the North East, erasing any preconceived notions of Scottish literature as a province solely concerned with bens, glens and romanticism. Kesson weaves poetry into prose and the Doric dialect into conventional narration, maintaining and justifying the description of her art as 'a skilful distillation of fact and fiction'.

Somewhere Beyond offers a selection of short stories, poems and works for radio spanning fifty years which continues this blending of autobiography and art. In her introduction to the volume, Isobel Murray identifies a way of reading Kesson's work as 'a series of exorcisms' created to express 'the pain and the excitement and the happiness of a lost past'. This collection is redolent with the agony of a traumatic childhood spent in various institutions. Yet it is triumphant too in its creation of continuity amidst these upheavals, in its vision of a community of 'ootlins' singing out their own truths in their own dialect.

Catherine McDonald

Anne Carson — *Men in the Off Hours*
Jonathan Cape pbk £10.00
ISBN 0-224-06104-6

This book is a catalogue of errors. But since that is how Carson defines poetry itself in 'Essay on What I Think About Most'—'the willful [sic] creation of error, / the deliberate break and complication of mistakes' —this is also a remarkable and frequently wonderful collection. These poems are suffused with a lightness of touch, a sense of humour, and a range of reference which lift them from the mundane, even where their theme is precisely the everyday and the worldly.

Carson rewrites mimesis, with reference to Aristotle, in terms of the disjunction between terms rather than their similarity, and in doing so makes irony, or perhaps even catachresis, the dominant mode of her work. Her models are classical poets whose work exists for us only in pieces, and she twice engages in exegesis of fragmentary verses, in which she refuses to reconstitute a putative intention behind the lines, or to 'reduce all textual delight / to an accident of history.' In doing so Carson makes a virtue of contingency: 'From the true mistakes of metaphor a lesson can be learned.'

Accordingly both the form and the themes of Carson's writing could be read in terms of her 'true mistakes.' The collection includes first and second drafts of poems which share titles, but little else; we find Virginia Woolf paired with Thucydides, first in a short introductory essay, and then in dialogue on the set of a television production of the Peloponnesian War; lines from Augustine set against poems derived from Edward Hopper paintings; a poem constructed as a dialogue with lines from Emily Dickinson's letters.

But listing Carson's poetic devices does not do her work justice. For the collection is intimately bound together, beyond the unexpected conjunctions which first strike the reader. Textual details recur: Emily Dickinson reappears in a later poem; Freud is a regular reference point; and classical literature is present throughout. (Perhaps inevitably. Carson teaches Classics at McGill University in Montreal, which is dealt with in what is certainly the funniest work on academic life I've ever read, 'Irony Is Not Enough: Essay on My Life as Catherine Deneuve.')

Thematically too, the collection is tautly woven. Error as a theme is subsumed into an experience of time as absence—the 'Off Hours' of the title. The curious null-time of

Hopper's paintings, a drawn-out extended present ('past and future circle round us') is matched with passages from Augustine's Confessions: 'But let us say / time present were long / because it was present it was long.' Specifically, Carson situates this as the moment of a war's beginning, an apparent commencement which is really an experience of waiting. The moment of action, time for the 'off,' is simultaneously the suspension of action and of temporality, the extended time which is not time, but 'off hours.' This is also an experience of time which is fundamentally gendered. 'Even in the off hours,' Carson writes, 'men know marks.'

Finally, however, it seems apt to read *Men in the Off Hours* as a work of mourning. Scattered throughout are epitaphs, culminating with one for Carson's mother. Typically, this consists of some crossed-out lines from the manuscript of Virginia Woolf's *Women and Fiction*, with their marginal annotation. It is an indication of the collection's success that this personal detail fails entirely to close down the meaning of the work, but instead opens it out further.

Alex Thomson

Valerie Thornton —
Catacoustics
Mariscat pbk £5
ISBN 0 946588 25 2

Brian Whittingham —
The Old Man from Brooklyn &
the Charing Cross Carpet
Mariscat pbk £5
ISBN 0 946588 23 6

Gael Turnbull — *Might a*
Shape of Words and other
transmutations
Mariscat pbk £5
ISBN 0 946588 24 4

The Mariscat Press, founded in 1982, is based in Glasgow, and specialises in the publication of the work of Scottish poets.

In Valerie Thornton's *Catacoustics*, the poetry switches between contrasting spaces, from familiar flats reverberating with the thrumming cats of her title, to the gusty countryside, backdrop to descriptions of the minutiae of wild things: segments of the bodies of insects; various bits of birds of prey. Thornton is a tutor of creative writing, and much of this collection could serve as exempla to her students: her poetry is competent and her imagery efficient. Curiously, her delicacy of description works best when riskily applied to the indelicacies of a different space: the urban landscape. Glimpses of Glasgow's 'tenement canyons', its shipyard's 'drooling chains' and a Jaipur sunset on the sandstone facades of Partick, achieve a visual power more messily resonant with a sense of place than the efficient and exemplary.

If Valerie Thornton works with visuals, Brian Whittingham's poetry in *The Old Man from Brooklyn & the Charing Cross Carpet* finds its effects in the oral and the aural. This is a hugely accomplished collection, and a collection in its true sense: the poems work with and against each other to produce a satisfying whole. As the duality of the title suggests, Whittingham has accumulated moments from each side of the Atlantic, as Glasgow and New York are linked and opposed by their human urban outcasts, and Scotland and America are compared and contrasted with reference to their native biting insects. 'I'd found people OK,' the narrator tells the eponymous old man, in response to complaints about the demise of the neighbourhood, and this observation could serve as the epigraph to the book. In these poems, people are OK, but weird, and some more so (on both counts) than others. Whittingham frequently builds a descriptive narrative and then interjects direct speech, and in the American poems these voices are fashioned to create distance, difference. The beer that the narrator is served with by the old man from Brooklyn is 'chilled/to suit the American palette', and the American idiom is a taste not quite acquired, even when in the mouths of Scots, as in 'The Argyle Street Evangelists'. In contrast, the Scots vernacular, when evoked, draws the reader into the poems, deflating the poetic, but heightening the pathos and the fun. For example, 'In Glasgow the Poet was a Snowflake', a precise description of some poor soul suffering for his performance art in a shopping street, ends: 'a young family was seen to walk away/shaking their heads/the father saying to the mother/an know what the best of it all is/they'll get fuckin paid fur that'. Likewise, in 'The Balance of Power', an American mosquito's anatomy catalogued in a scientific tome is juxtaposed with 'The Scottish Midge/A dipterous insect', the description of which is rendered in the visceral vernacular: 'A wee fuckin nyaff/that buzzes aboot yir napper/ bitin an nibblin/leavin totey red spots oan yir skin/an generally hee-haw good tae man nor beast'. (A mock foot-note traces a similar balance of power in the Scottish Air Force Elite's forthcoming strategic fighter plane.)

The eponymous poem from the eastern shores of the Atlantic tells of a staggering man weaving home after hours who discovers a soiled 'magic' carpet outside a refurbished Indian restaurant, and flies back to Castlemilk on it. For Brian Whittingham, the realist magic of his native land is infinitely more inspirational than the tinny, shiny spells of the USA.

Gael Turnbull's *Might a Shape of Words* consists, he claims at the end of his collection, of 'elements of transformation and mutation, and of other texts, even sometimes abandoned fragments of my own'. Rather than poetry per se, then, each page contains a 'shape of words', each with the air of a metaphysical anecdote, an illustration of a 'great truth'. The personae of these anecdotes are occasionally specific ('a young mother'), but more often vague ('a woman', 'a boy', a writer). Most interesting are those built around the central, carefully universal 'he', which hymn the impossibility of a solution, a reconciliation, for a life already lived. A man walking alone on a beach 'thinks of nothing/except the most intolerable of paradoxes: to dread everything closing in when it is the emptiness of the world which baffles'. The word 'paradox' is repeated elsewhere, also in a context tinged with paranoia, and it is tempting to read this voice as that of the author, a voice attempting to come to terms with the onset of old age. In these fragments, and others like them, the great truths remain stubbornly elusive, rehearsing and illustrating the thwarted quest of 'he'.

Perhaps our post-modern sensibilities are too accustomed to uncertainty, but when the anecdotes, as they do increasingly towards the end of the collection, conclude with a philosophical profundity, these conclusions jar with the arrogance of their conviction. No-one seems transformed, or transmuted, as promised: people are prompted to realise something that was always there, always true. Epiphanies, affecting when tantalisingly incomplete, are easy to weary of when recurrent and profound.

Alice Ferrebe

James Tait Black in brief

The James Tait Black Prizes for fiction and biography are awarded annually to what are judged— traditionally by the senior professor in the University of Edinburgh's Department of English Literature— to be the best works written in English and published in Britain in the previous year. The department receives over 200 submissions from publishers, all of which are read by a team of post-graduate volunteers. While only two works can be winners —this year Zadie Smith's *White Teeth* and Martin Amis' *Experience*—the readers' reports offer an insightful survey of the eclectic range of one year's nominations. Below we include a selection of some of the memorable comments on the good, the bad and the ugly of a year in British publishing.

Lesley and Roy Adkins, *The Keys of Egypt: The Race to Read the Hieroglyphs*
Harper Collins £16.99

Occasionally repetitive and with some peculiar chronology, *The Keys of Egypt* is nonetheless readable, accessible, and a worthwhile popular history that successfully uses biography as a way into scientific history.

Martin Amis, *Experience*
Vintage £7.99

Unlike many biographies, which combine scholarly precision and scope with a deadening mode of omniscient 'realist' narration, this is a fully writerly book. Purposefully unorthodox in its reinvention of the genre, it doesn't so much use it as

dance with it.

Noel Annan, *The Dons: Mentors, Eccentrics and Geniuses*
Harper Collins £7.99

Its nostalgic tone does little to conceal that this book is a memorial to an Oxbridge world—and a wider world—which Annan thinks has given way to one of league tables and standardised assessments. An amusing obituary of the old-fashioned don.

Kate Atkinson, *Emotionally Weird*
Black Swan £4.99

Atkinson deftly interweaves various different genres and narratives—campus satire, family history and cheap detective fiction— in this genuinely funny novel.

Imogen de la Bere, *The Understanding of Jenner Ransfield*
Vintage £6.99

Colourful and deeply entertaining account of young Theodora Potts' encounter with Dr Jenner Ransfield, an expert in the field of bull semen.

**Miles Bredin, *The Pale Abyssinian: A Life of James Bruce, African Explorer and Adventurer*
Flamingo £7.99**

This is an excellent and entertaining account of the Scottish explorer, with a picaresque narrative that suits its subject perfectly.

**Kathleen Burk, *Troublemaker: The Life and History of A.J.P. Taylor*
Yale UP £20**

This comprehensive and precise study is alert to causal patterns and processes in a way that Taylor himself would have appreciated. Enjoyably, it provides an excellent balance of accurate research, entertaining prose and illuminating anecdote.

**John Burnside, *Burning Elvis*
Jonathan Cape £10**

These stories read like the work of a poet, but compared with Burnside's poetry these are mechanical exercises. The icons of modern cultural panic fail to substitute for emotional authenticity.

**A.S. Byatt, *The Biographer's Tale*
Chatto & Windus £15.99**

This is highly professional literary fiction which fails to live up to its own premises: disillusioned postgraduate ditches literary theory for a biography of a biographer but ends up studying stag beetles instead.

**Matthew Fitt, *But & Ben A-Go-Go*
Luath Press £10.99**

Sadly, the exhilarating use of Scots in Fitt's first novel is neatly matched by the author's poverty of imagination, so the book has none of the sparkle of Edwin Morgan's sci-fi work or of *A Voyage to Arcturus*, surely the Scottish classic in the genre.

**Leslie Forbes, *Fish, Blood and Bones*
Phoenix £6.99**

This is the kind of book every judge secretly craves—the truly dreadful novel that can be cheerfully abandoned halfway through. Forbes' so-called thriller commits the cardinal sin of its genre, by failing to provide any excitement whatsoever.

Jane Gardham, *The Flight of the Maidens*
Chatto & Windus, £15.99

This novel kept almost saying that the war was good for young women as it gave them opportunities they would never otherwise have had, liberated them sexually to a certain extent, and freed them from expectations of impending marriage, but never quite dared to do so. I wish it had, but it preferred instead to emulate the seering social realism of Jilly Cooper's work.

Claire Harman, *Fanny Burney: A biography*
Harper Collins £8.99

An excellent biography dealing intelligently with the difficulty of writing about Burney and her family, themselves compulsive writers and re-writers of their own lives.

Shirley Hazzard, *Greene on Capri: A Memoir*
Virago £6.99

This is a very slim volume with very slender ambitions and almost anorexic achievements. Poorly written, oddly punctuated and of no interest beyond the anecdotal.

John Kelly, *The Little Hammer*
Vintage £6.99

A promising first novel, centring on an Irish painter and his childhood memories of saints, murder and palaeontology. We're used to—and perhaps even bored of—the old unreliable narrator trope and dark suppressed childhood memories, but Kelly's writing possesses a deftness that saves this novel from cliché.

John King, *Human Punk*
Vintage £6.99

All the boys wear Dr Marten boots, and put these boots 'in' whenever possible. And we are informed of every single record they listen to, because as the narrator tells us, it's 'the soundtrack of your life'. Or rather, a way of establishing cheap nostalgia without having to do any creative writing for it.

John Maurice, *Jabberwocky Day*
Book Guild Ltd, £15.95

Alternatively tries to be all *à la* Le Carré in its portentous (or is it pretentious?) simplicity and all John Fowles in its mythic dreaminess. Our mysterious commentator says at one point 'There are reasons for writing all this down which escape me...' Me too.

Isobel Murray, *Jessie Kesson: Writing her life*
Canongate £12.99

This first biography of Jessie Kesson is hugely disappointing. Murray has failed to deal with the primary problem and fascination of writing about Kesson—that she continually wrote, rewrote and imagined her life in her writings.

Tim Pears, *A Revolution of the Sun*
Black Swan £6.99

Trying to make his enormous cast of characters memorable, Pears has to resort to two tactics: short-hand 'types', or people with histories so bizarre they lose all credibility.

Amy Phillips, *Enveloped: Desire … Disordered*
Pentland Press £10.50

The major weakness of Phillips' autobiography is that it seeks to describe her experience in terms taken from the tired language of confessional television and popular therapy. Consequently, what is a highly private series of disclosures reads in a highly impersonal way.

Edward Platt, *Leadville: A biography of the A40*
Picador £9.99

Leadville is inevitably a mongrel of a book—part Sunday supplement, part anti-car polemic, part George Orwell—it is also fascinating and always readable, and indeed a biography of a road.

Donald Rawley, *The End of Miss Kind*
Flamingo £9.99

A tautly-written and engaging thriller with something of the prose style and worldliness of Alex Trocchi, this was published posthumously and reads like the work of a dying man.

Ben Richards, *A Sweetheart Deal*
Headline Review £6.99

It's lauded on its cover as being a 'London' novel, which means a lot of place names and muted admiration of the shabby majesty of the city, which, as we all know, is the only place in the world with tower-blocks and sunsets and nutters on the streets.

Alexei Sayle, *Barcelona Plates*
Sceptre £6.99

Sayle would seem to be another example of a good comedian desperate to become a bad writer.

Alexander McCall Smith, *Tears of the Giraffe*
Edinburgh UP £8.99

This is a superior piece of detective fiction, written in simple, direct but effective prose. Perhaps most importantly, this novel offers a refreshingly positive picture of an African nation—and probably deserves a wide audience in the West on those grounds alone.

Zadie Smith, *White Teeth*
Penguin £5.99

The heterogeneity of the British racial mix is rivalled only by the span of knowledge apparent in the book: taking in the history of Empire, genetic engineering, numerous world religions and the process of straightening afro hair. Smith plots tightly amidst an impressively wide time-scale—that the novel holds triumphantly together with this span is testament to her precocious accomplishment.

Brian Thompson, *A Monkey Among Crocodiles: The Disastrous Life of Mrs Georgina Weldon*
Harper Collins £8.99

Apparently a rare copy of Georgina Weldon's memoirs came to Brian Thompson's attention by complete accident—it 'bobbed to the surface' he writes—if only he had allowed it to sink again without trace.

Giles Waterfield, *The Long Afternoon*
Review £14.99

A stultifying and insular account of expatriate life in the South of France before the second world war. This novel is based around the author's own family experiences, which means that any whiff of social satire is ironically defused.

Christoph Wolff, *Johann Sebastian Bach: The Learned Musician*
Oxford UP £25

This biography focuses almost exclusively on jobs and money, with the unfortunate impression emerging that music is purely a business and that Bach's musical genius is best judged in terms of how much he was paid.

Subscribe to *Edinburgh Review*

SUBSCRIBING TO EDINBURGH REVIEW
- Guarantees delivery of the best new writing in Scotland, direct to your door.
- Brings you the best new critical thought in Britain.
- Keeps you informed about the latest work from the small press world.
- Ensures you receive all three issues a year.
- Is still cheaper than buying the magazine in a bookshop.
- Costs only £17 a year for individuals, £34 for institutions.

BACK ISSUES are also available at a discount rate, please contact our office for more information or to place an order.

SUBSCRIPTION FORM

Name:
Address:

Postcode:

I wish to subscribe to the Edinburgh Review, beginning from issue 107 / ___ .

- * I enclose a cheque made for £17 (individual) / £34 (institutional) made payable to 'Edinburgh Review'
- * I wish to pay by Credit / Debit Card, details below:
  [* = delete as applicable]
     Type of Card: VISA / Mastercard / Switch [Delete as appropriate]
     Card Number:
     Card Valid from: _ / _ / _ To: _ / _ / _ Issue No: _ [Switch Only]

Signature:_____   Date: _ / _ / _

Please complete and return form to Edinburgh Review, 22a Buccleuch Place, Edinburgh, EH8 9LN